Contents

Foreword

Media Ethics and the Technological Society

For French thinker Jacques Ellul, the transition to a technological society is more fundamental than anything the human race has experienced for thousands of years. Originally organized around nature, for centuries human society has served as the cosmic axis. In the Western experience, the PreSocratics—Thales, Anaximander, Anaximenes—debated earth, air, fire, and water as origins one of the other, until Socrates made humans the centerpiece.

The technological world now is effacing these two orders. Nature and society have become secondary environments. They no longer decide our future. They are subordinate and not basic. In Jean Baudrillard's simulacra of images, electronic networks, and cybernetic models, hyper-reality becomes reality itself.

Although technologies have always been used, we are now in a quantum shift to another order of magnitude. The issue for Ellul is not a proliferation of technologies one by one but a technological organism. His major books speak of an epoch: *The Technological Society* and *The Technological System*. Technology in industrial societies is the locus of value now as capital was for Marx. Although civilizations across the centuries have invented tools, a qualitative shift has occurred in the 20th century. Ellul refers to Engel's law: As quantity increases quality changes. A town of 1,000 is on a continuum of numbers to a city of 1,000,000. However, along the trajectory, a fundamental shift occurs so that a major urban center is radically different from a rural village.

Unlike previous eras in which tools are constrained within a larger complex of social values, the pervasiveness and sophistication of modern techniques reorganizes society to conform to their demand for efficiency. Scientific techniques are applied not just to nature but to social organizations and our understanding of personhood. The everyday has a mechanical cadence. In Ellul's terms, modern society has sacralized the genius behind machines and uncritically allowed its rampaging power to infect not just industry, engineering, and business but also politics, education, the church, labor unions, and international relations. Unable to establish a meaningful life outside the artificial ambiance of a technocratic culture, human beings place their ultimate hope in it. Seeing no other source of security, we tend to become slaves to technical productivity. Moral purpose is sacrificed to technological excellence.

In the classic case of the tomato picker designed by the University of California–Irvine, a new hybrid tomato had to be developed—tough skins so they would not break, tomatoes that all ripened at the same time with chemical color added as necessary, and tomatoes square or oblong so they moved on feeding trays better. Adapting the tomato to the machine is an analogue of Ellul's concern in the technological society. Relentlessly and overwhelmingly, an instrumental mentality preempts human existence for itself.

The question, then, is not whether technical means can be analyzed but the more complicated problem of world views. Machineness, efficiency, and the mystique of technique eat into our deepest being—our philosophy of life. The technological order is so pervasive, so overwhelming in its ubiquity, we can contain it no longer. Of course, an unending list of short-term crises demands our attention also, but our major worry long term ought to be our attenuated philosophy of life. The instrumentalist worldview is invading our spirit, and influencing the way we teach and learn, and managing our social institutions. A calculus of averages and probabilities is replacing ends, the common good, and distributive justice; the technological order is reconstituting the moral order in terms of technique.

Media technologies are implicated fully. The principle of efficiency that characterizes the technological enterprise as a whole also dominates the communications apparatus; the media do not transmit neutral data but integrate us into the overall system. In Ellul's framework, communications media represent the meaning edge of the technological system. Information systems incarnate the properties of technology while serving as the agents for interpreting the very phenomenon they embody. For Ellul, communication systems are the innermost and most elusive manifestation of human technological activity. As the mass media sketch out our world for us, organize our conversations, determine our decisions, and influence our self-identities, they do so with a technological rhythm.

In working on an ethics of new media technologies, we do not have the luxury of dealing with the internet, digital communications, computer storage systems, satellite transmission, and so forth in isolation. We need, instead, sophisticated social ethics to match the power of our instrumental era. Modern technology has introduced such novel scales and consequences that the framework of traditional ethics no longer addresses them. Given the explosive and largely unknown effects of technological innovation, for example, consequentialist ethics on the whole are irrelevant. Moreover, the incredible development of technology in the professions is radically transforming their structure and practice. Our models of professional responsibility built on informed consent, whistle blowing, contract duties, and rights do not speak to the conditions of a global communications order.

Therefore, in this special issue on ethics and the new technologies, the framework throughout is sociological. The orientation is not, first of all, individual autonomy, professional codes of ethics, and utility. The context is the technological society. Thomas W. Cooper's encyclopedia of ethical issues is shaped in its categories and definitions by the social effects of the new technologies. Adam Clayton Powell III develops one of those categories, satellite technology, in terms of sociopolitical observation rather than micro-privacy protection. Donald B. Kraybill uses historical sociology to flesh out ethical objections to television and the internet. David J. Gunkel situates the texts and technologies of cyberspace within cultural politics and the ideology of dualism.

With Cooper staking out the agenda, three ways to implement it are illustrated here. Each of the forty issues—and others from his expanding repertoire—warrant in-depth treatment. In the tradition of Lewis Mumford, historical understanding of our social struggles with technology is vital; cultures not embracing high tech stimulate our thinking. Philosophical analysis of the underlying assumptions regarding knowledge, reality, humanity, and values are an ongoing necessity, too.

On another level, as signposts, these ethical forays into the technological society's newest media indicate the sociological direction in which communication ethics should go conceptually. They serve as a reminder of the normative core this field will need to stay on track. With the new media technologies understood as a social necessity, their axis is distributive justice. Media ethics in confronting the digital convergence of information technologies calls for a radical shift from the criterion of mechanical efficiency to an ethics of social justice. The master principle of this model is allocating to everyone according to essential needs, regardless of income or geographical location. Our task in media ethics is critical reflection without stepping outside the big picture—ethical principles developed interactively with the technological order. Particular guidelines as we construct them close to the bone of everyday crises are not added up brick by brick toward an ill-defined aggregate, but they illuminate a social ethics model rooted in distributive justice. A need-based social justice serves like an ancient cornerstone of the media ethics building in the technological era, squaring up the lines and anchoring its architectural contours.

Basic human needs related to survival or subsistence are categorically different from frivolous wants or individual whims. Agreement is rather uniform on most fundamental issues such as food, housing, safety, and medical care. All are entitled—without regard for individual success—to what permits them to live humanely. The future electronic superhighway cannot be envisioned except as a necessity. Information networks will make police and fire protection available, give us access to health care and the library, organize world trade, and serve as the avenue through which we vote and discuss political issues. Therefore, as a necessity of life, the information system in industrial economies of the future ought to be distributed impartially, regardless of income or geographical location.

However, there is no reasonable likelihood that a need-based version of social justice will ever be fulfilled by the commercial sector. This ethical theory requires that we find ways in legislation, public policy, and public ownership to implement it. Our approach to media institutions should be modeled after schools, which we accept as our common public responsibility, rather than determined by engineers or by profits alone.

Suppose one agrees that a need-based conception of justice is preferable to the instrumentalism that dominates our thinking now. Suppose further, as is likely, that the perfect achievement of equal access is impossible, given the realities of finite financial and technological resources. At this point the guideline of similar treatment for similar cases becomes important. If we simply cannot provide a sophisticated level of service for all, it is more just to discriminate by categories of service rather than between the information rich and information poor. All homes, for instance, should have fire and police view-data capability, rather than some homes having every convenience and others receiving no services. The formula of similar treatment for similar cases modifies the way a need-conception of justice is applied in a real world of constraints. Rather than a wholesale commitment to efficiency, distributive justice requires that we slow the pace of the information society and continually promote alternative small-scale technology as the essential needs of all require it.

Instead of allowing engineers to design a global system using the norm of efficiency, or encouraging companies to compete for it on the basis of profitability, the ethical principle of distributive justice should be up front—at the vortex of the information revolution. Over the long-term, everyone will benefit the most worldwide if social justice is on the cutting edge in these heady transition days from the Industrial Age to the Information Age.

Clifford Christians
Guest Editor

Journal of Mass Media Ethics
Volume 13, Number 2, pp. 71–92

New Technology Effects Inventory: Forty Leading Ethical Issues

By Thomas W. Cooper

Emerson College

❑*Arguably, every new technology creates hidden effects in its environment, rearranging the social order it penetrates. Many of these effects are inextricably linked to ethical issues. Some are eternal issues such as censorship and free speech, but others have new names and dimensions, and may even be new issues. Forty of these issues pertaining to the new communication technologies of the 1990s and next millennium are catalogued here. The author argues that each new communication technology either retrieves, amplifies, transforms, obsolesces, or mixes ethical issues from the past or creates new issues for the future. However, as in the Ross Hume Hall (1974) effect, it is also likely there are issues yet unknown due to untested effects of combining new technologies.*

A ripple effect is changed by what produces the ripple. Dropping a stone into a pond usually produces a steady, predictable pattern. However, dropping an opened can of paint leaves an unpredictable color design. Dropping two moving motorboats with twin propellers creates a different, changing pattern, and dropping a nuclear bomb may alter the entire ecosystem and even ripple speed.

Similarly, introducing one new technology into society may produce a seemingly predictable ripple pattern of effects, at least on the surface. Another new technology will act differently and raise unforeseen social and ethical issues. To further complicate matters, introducing technologies into different countries and cultures produces patterns as different as dropping unlit fireworks into a pond and into a fire. The nature of the technology, who has access to it, and the context into which it is introduced may greatly alter its impact on society.

McLuhan (1964) noted that a bomber pilot is totally detached from the disruption and rearrangement of lives, families, and businesses caused by the bombs below. Likewise, creators of technologies have little awareness of how their inventions are the catalyst for social, cultural, political, and economic changes. Scant attention is given to the ethical issues, side effects, and concomitant transformations that accompany inventions until after widespread implementation with unexpected results.

For these and many other reasons, it is important to study each new technology before and during its introduction into countries, tribes, businesses, schools, and neighborhoods. Hidden effects and ethical issues discovered after the fact have led to confusion, frustration, social dilemmas, and corporate lawsuits. Because new communication and information technologies are being introduced more rapidly into society than ever before, and into some societies for the first time, it is especially important to study the effects and ethical issues accompanying new communications media.

Computers, satellites, fiber optics, faxes, the internet, virtual reality, and a host of other technologies have sustained, amplified, transformed, and introduced numerous ethical issues and social effects before society can predict or digest such rapid change. In a runaway technology and effect explosion, it is natural for humanity to wish to regain dominion over technology and its effects. Appropriately enough, an International Radio and Television Society (IRTS) thinker (Kohler, 1997) created an imaginary American media company called Dominion in his case study for a 1997 IRTS seminar in New York. Within the case study, teams of university professors who simulated the roles of company executives and managers were asked to research how this largely traditional media company (Dominion) might introduce new technology products and services into its company vision and sales over the next 5 years.

This article suggests the types of ethical issues and related social effects a company like Dominion might face when implementing and distributing new technology products and services. Indeed the following inventory is also a partial list of issues and effects already encountered by real companies, institutions, governments, and other organizations.[1]

Issues and Effects

1. *Agency:* Intelligent agents are sophisticated cyber "worker bees" who labor around the clock to perform secretarial, library, and other tasks as programmed by their user. Agency implies all the ethical issues surrounding electronic substitutions for person-to-person contact including impersonal, redundant, unthinking action performed or mailed "on behalf of." Agency connotes the insensitivity to human pain, purpose, and perception portrayed by HAL, the computer in *2001: A Space Odyssey* (Kubrick, 1968).

2. *Anonymity:* Many electronic message systems make false, borrowed, encrypted, and unknown identities (fake IDs) easier to transmit further, faster, and en masse. Not only do problems of deception and secrecy multiply, but e-mail bombs, viruses, harassment, laundered money, invasion of privacy, libel, obscenity, and other ethical problems become more tempting and widespread when the user's true identity is hidden (Singer, 1996).

3. *Autism:* Metaphorically, an autistic society wears headsets, virtual reality headgear, and a wraparound "wired womb," protecting itself against a threatening reality. Phasing out human contact in favor of electronic surround, the "Rainman" culture creates more communication consumption machines than children, and American children absorb more recycled ads, shows, pop hits, video games, and software violence than fresh air and fresh ideas (Cooper, 1986–1987, 1997).

4. *Automation:* Although replacing skilled craftsmen with machines has been common practice for decades, cyber automation features new software every month that renders skills and trades obsolete or less necessary. Downsizing, layoffs, and corporate and institutional restructuring are common features of the omnitransformative age. Automation also transforms consciousness and reinforces social dependency on technology and "techne" (Ellul, 1964; Mumford, 1956, 1962).

> **Standards become impossible . . . when . . . participants have no central control point.**

5. *Bootlegging:* Copying, selling and reselling other people's software, tapes, CDs, data, and other forms of information becomes instant in an age of point-and-click duplicating, xerography, and home copying. Further complicating these matters are diverse definitions and standards regarding ownership, information flow, piracy, and intellectual property across cultural and national boundaries (Barlow, 1996).

6. *Codes of ethics:* Codes, guidelines, norms, standards, policies for internet, and cyberspace practice become impossible to implement when the technologies, participants, servers, and vendors in a global (multi-) medium represent numerous languages, ethical mores, and transient sites with no central control point. Even more difficult to standardize and implement are guidelines for brushfire technologies, which spread quickly one after another, often interact, and become quickly dated or obsolete.

7. *Confidentiality—sources—secrecy:* Age-old problems of containment are magnified in an age of electronic encryption, interception, and the ongoing battle of codemakers versus codebreakers. Anonymous sources become more plentiful and difficult to identity when pseudosites, third-party location, "carriers," mobile cellular phones, online covers, and impersonation further conceal the identity, locale, gender, and personality of the messenger.

8) *Conflict of interest:* Major mergers feature old media (broadcasting, print) holding hands with new, such that fewer and fewer players control large corridors of information. Increasingly, owners have conflicting inter-

ests in the operations of new media and multiplesystems. As broadcasters and studios merge with multiple systems (Time—Warner—Turner) or with software providers (MSNBC) or with telephony (Bell Atlantic—TCI) the question "in whose interest?" is more frequently asked about telecommunication and new tech operations and acquisitions.

9. *Consumerism—commercialization—materialism:* New technologies often import advertising, urban rhythms, and the accompanying vision of a lavish lifestyle. Sukarno (McLuhan, 1975) regarded the influx of Hollywood into Indonesia as "a monster ad for consumer goods." Even the presence of the internet in some regions is an indirect ad for computers, software, video games, and a high-tech vogue. More than any preceding communication technologies, those of the 1990s and of the new millennium are themselves consumable—throw-away cameras, quickly dated software, and last year's hardware. Nothing is obsolete until you own it.

10. *Cultural erosion:* Both tribes and anthropologists have seen communication technologies as a factor in the erosion of authentic tribal traditions and customs. Ogden's (1991) observation about the effects of headsets and television in the Marshall Islands is echoed in the sentiments of Ereira and Mystic Fire Corp.'s (1991) *The Elder Brother's Warning.* Pavlik (1996) noted the bans by China, Saudi Arabia, and other Muslim countries on satellite dishes. Desacrelization, obscenity, and the homogenization of culture are common fears. Satellite footprint overspill, internet invasion, and Madison Avenue exportation into tiny islands like Yap mix the Playboy channel with the Koran–Bible belt (Yap, 1987).

11. *Deception:* Numerous ethical problems such as digital manipulation, impersonation, false advertising, puffery, hype, masking, and data massaging abound. The deliberate and accidental substitution of illusion for reality, and propaganda for proper data, have become far easier. Documents may be altered without detection by long-distance ghosts and realistic, albeit artificial, images may be quickly synthesized. Theoretically, a presidential candidate may now be computer generated, credentialed online, and elected without ever being publicly seen (other than via a human stand-in).

12. *Defamation (slander and libel):* Character assassination may be orchestrated by innumerable electronic agents generating anonymous smear campaigns. Internet servers who provide wires for libelous accusations about real people are, or are not, accountable for said content depending on technology, culture, and location. Questions about responsibility and accountability for content magnify. Are the damages against a person's reputation published in a newspaper less significant if published online in the more malleable, nonmass medium of the internet?

13. *Dehumanization:* Robots and artificial intelligence have long been viewed as the antithesis to humanity and, thus, a threat to human values. However, 900 numbers, virtual mates, and cyber pets now seem more threatening to human relationships. How may spouses compare sexually to a perfect, life-size image that never complains and simulates all sensual pleasures without aging, gaining weight, or crying? Humans increasingly imitate such icons through cosmetics, silicon implants, surgery, and so forth (Mitroff & Bennis, 1989).

14. *Democracy—governance:* Elections are increasingly controlled by those who own or buy time on major media. Satellites and fiber-optic cables make possible the Big Brother possibilities of Orwell (1949) in a world in which all stations may receive a single signal via omniconferencing and cybercommunity. New surveillance technologies also make possible a world in which all "dangerous" citizens are observed and potentially reported or controlled. Although many new technologies are decentralized and liberating, they also make possible the concentration of power into the hands of a few megahackers who quietly change data and history, eliminate powerpoints via hypervirus, or empower Big Brother via exclusively owned super-SATAN software and its kin.

15. *Destructive applications:* Although new technologies advance unprecedented levels of weapon development and evolution, a greater destructive capability exists in the lack of control over weapons already existing. World War III will not be won by those with superior weapons but by those who may use remote cyber-controls to turn weapons back on those who fired them (and who become boomerang targets). All systems dependent on artificial intelligence—air traffic control, world bank, power companies, nuclear reactor functions—may also be destroyed by the abuse or destruction of artificial intelligence.

16. *Digital manipulation:* As Arnheim (1971) argued in the 1920s, the more a technology resembles reality, the greater the possibility it can be distorted to mislead us. Scitex, CEPS, and Adobe programs that allow adjustment of hue, shape, and saturation of individual pixels, usher in the age of morphing and visual cloning. Powell (1994) predicted totally synthetic news events and Pavlik (1996) noted a manipulated Pulitzer Prize winning retouched photo. Questions of verisimilitude versus reality, fakery versus spoofing and parody, and racism (the O.J. Simpson *Time* cover) versus realism run rampant.

17. *Environmental damage—waste:* Large amounts of chemical by-products, toxic waste, resource depletion, and environmental imbalance result from the production, distribution, and utilization of new technologies. More oil (petroleum-based ink) may have been spilled writing about the Exxon

Valdez than by the event. Daily use of computer and newspaper destroys forests, and the earth now wears a giant, radiant electric blanket. Fiber optics, refractory coating, satellite parking lots, suboceanic dredging to lay cable, not to mention plastic manufacturing and waste, all add to the coming state of what scientists call *omnicide*, the death of all life as we know it.

18. *Fairness—equality:* One of the most ancient ethical issues is magnified when discussing resources (technology rich and technology poor countries, regions, and peoples), access, and even air space. Questions about how the air spectrum should be allocated, about whether foreign owned satellites may orbit over domestic military sites, about who should be charged and how much for transmission and transponder time magnify questions of global equality, inequality, and fairness. Similarly, questions of intellectual property, ownership, royalties, and so forth raise questions of distributive justice. Who, if anyone, should profit from the distribution of information?

19. *Flaming and internet—telecom protocol:* New technologies introduce a new vocabulary such as *flaming*, *spamming*, and *slamming* that summon up old vocabulary such as *rudeness*, *crudeness*, and *imposition*. Flaming (sending negative feedback, criticism, even mailbombing to quiet unwanted advertising or problematic e-mail on the net), spamming (sending out unwanted cyberadvertising), and mailbombing (targeting and taking out specific computers by mail overload or cybersabotage), albeit often unethical, may often be defended as a response to unethical communication (Pavlik, 1996).

20. *Freedom of expression—censorship:* Recent controversy over whether the press should have access to military satellite information sparked a traditional press versus Pentagon tug of war. First Amendment battles rage around the limits to internet censorship without which library computers are jammed by teens and children finding online pornography. Although the controversy has always brewed at the microlevel, home movies mixed with multimedia make almost everyone a potential hate mail, pedophilia, or psychotic mass message merchant from one's own home.

21. *Gender and race:* The open and decentralized nature of the internet has permitted many hate sites, gender biased chatgroups, Holocaust denial locales, and so forth. Online racism, harassment, obscene *eel* (e-mail) calls, are encouraged by the distant proximity, anonymity, ubiquity, and convenience of cyberports, public fax machines, the World Wide Web, and a wired and cable world. Whether cyberhate, sexist bulletin boards, and online ethnic wars may be limited is a function of local policies, national laws, international agreements, and especially the implementation of all of those.

22. *Hidden taping—tapping:* Wire-tapping and taping have moved toward hidden monitoring of data transactions. Ludlow (1996) reported that the U.S. government, for example, is making inroads at observing individual electronic cash flow. Most e-mail users are unaware of whether their provider, their employer, or their local gatekeeper can read their e-mail. Because e-mail, faxes, and so forth, unlike telephony and telegraphy, automatically are recorded messages, their duplication, forwarding, preservation, and delayed monitoring become far easier.

23. *Impersonation:* Recently, a midwest coed left her computer so she could run an errand and returned to find numerous X-rated sexual come-ons in her e-mail. While she was away, a male prankster had sent out a hot sexual come-on from "her" to many locations by using her terminal and identity. Impersonation makes it possible for Saddam Hussein to take distance-learning courses in military strategy from West Point (or similar) or Howard Stern to earn a dozen online honors degrees (with the help of nerds using his name) from as many universities. The unethical and even criminal possibilities seem endless.

24. *Information flow—distribution:* Lamberton (1997) cited *asset egalitarianism* and *information asymmetry* as two problems in Australian telecommunication that echo worldwide. Governments, gatekeepers, corporations, and policies may promote either a one-, two-, or multiway flow of information. Although Barlow (1996) argued that information wants to be free, corporations argue that information wants to be profitable and seek to control it by trademark, copyright, access, and distribution. Garfinkel, Stallman, and Kapor (1996) documented how big fish (companies or countries) swallow little fish (companies or countries) in patent wars. Those who can mount the largest lawsuits, trade pressures, and competitive muscle often largely influence information flow, containment, and technology development dams.

25. *Information underclass:* Like cultural erosion, cultural dependency features dominant countries, corporations, and groups preying on the economies, resources, and markets of underclass countries, often in return for access to technology and services. The information haves (often First and Second World countries) and have nots (often Third World countries) are further reinforced by the growth of cyber literacy among the former and cyber illiteracy, and often technology deprivation, among the second. Questions about fairness, justice, democracy, and access are abundant.

26. *Insufficient testing:* Tunnel vision, bottom-line mentality, competitive rush, and downsizing economics are some of the factors that lead manufacturers, inventors, governments, and venture capitalists to overlook the thorough independent pretesting and follow-up testing necessary with new

communication and information technologies. Although it would be unthinkable to dissolve the Federal Food and Drug Administration which pretests new foods and drugs for side effects before they are marketed and sold, the U.S. government abolished the Office of Technology Assessment, which was already minuscule in comparison to the large number of new inventions and media. In-company research often fails to protect the consumer, as tobacco company research illustrates.

27. *Intellectual property—ownership:* Copyright and patent abuse have become the 1990s nightmare. Both laws and ethics vary from country to country, medium to medium, and subculture to subculture, and those who implement policies and legislation cannot keep up with brushfire technologies. Therefore, ethical and epistemological questions springing from "what is an idea?" and "to whom, if anyone, does it belong?" magnify, especially when so many microproducts (cf. software) are clusters of patented segments. Implementation within an ocean of new, tiny, instantly transportable products is a second nightmare (Barlow, 1996; Godwin, 1996; Heckel, 1996; Ludlow, 1996).

> **Questions about fairness, justice, democracy, and access are abundant.**

28. *Macro issues:* At the macro level, environmentalists seem to argue more about when than if the world will end. Single technologies like the telephone, which necessitate small forests of telephone poles and larger forests of huge, seldom-used telephone books in each city and megatons of copper and plastic worldwide, contribute to such macro issues as terrahomicide. Other macro issues include the widespread vacuum of thought about the larger impact of multitechnology on human thinking and activity, interactivity, the Ross Hume Hall (1974) effect (discussed under The New Factors later), the absence of greater purpose for many technologies (other than a Yuppie toy chest), and the Huxley/Postman syndrome, that we are amusing ourselves to death (Huxley, 1932; Postman, 1988).

29. *Mind control:* How are epistemology, consciousness, literacy, and general thought modes changed in an age when we see over 5,000 ads before we enter kindergarten, when journalism becomes brain surgery without a license, when point and click replace read and write, and when virtual becomes associated with reality? More education takes place outside than inside the classroom; the classroom, in turn, is infiltrated by commercialized, hip Channel One. This researcher has heard at least some educators report that the internet would be most often accessed for pornography, not

knowledge, if not patrolled and that spell check and Groliers CD-Rom replace skills and in-depth research. To what extent will the instant fix for answers replace reflective, multidocumented criticism and analysis?

30. *Monopoly—antitrust:* Bagdikian's (1997) theme that fewer and fewer hands control greater amounts of information becomes even more evident among the few digerati (cf. literati) at the top (e.g., the Microsoft–Netscape wars, the Bell Atlantic–TCI–Paramount finagling). Global super powers jockey for position via intermarriage and clan rivalries such that customers who seem to have greater choices via cable's many channels and the internet's content cornucopia actually have far fewer rivers into which these revenue streams flow. Major ethical issues revolve around the limits to (corporate) growth, public choice, multitongue voices (a la Rupert Murdoch), global dominance, single-source knowledge, and even content conversion— as in Pavlik's (1996) observation that when G.E. acquired NBC "news at any cost" (pp. 16–17) values were replaced with a strict bottom-line orientation (Bagdikian, 1997; Lamberton, 1997).

31. *Multiuser domain (MUD) abuse:* Pavlik (1996) described MUDs as "a broad class of online adventure games in which at least two participants play in fantasy worlds they help create" (p. 170). He further reported that they became so addictive that Amherst College banned them in 1992, and Australia banned them from the entire continent. MUDs are not only addictive, but often blur the line between fantasy violence and real violence. "Killing" someone in online "Dungeons and Dragons" seems paradoxically at once all the more harmless (because it is just a game) but all the more tempting (because one is so drawn in). MUD-related real-life violence, harassment, and animosity, sometimes by children, is a disturbing side effect of the "games" (cf. Curtis, 1996).

32. *Noise pollution:* Acoustic experts such as Schaeffer (1977) and listening specialists have reminded us that sound is not noise and that noise (unwanted or disturbing sound) has increased drastically in this century. Shannon and Weaver (1949), whose mathematical theory was one basis for the study of communication, defined noise more as meaningless, distracting, or disruptive sound (or visual static) that interfered with or overlaid the message. Both types of noise accompany the proliferation of technologies, new and old, and both confuse and annoy the learner, consumer, and even average citizen who may bemoan the absence of silence or the presence of glitches, background sounds, hissing, cyberconfusion, boom boxes, programmed music, and white noise in increasingly remote corridors.

33. *Obscenity—indecency—pornography:* So much is being written about the online obscenity debate that it is difficult to know whom to quote. U.S. legislation such as the Exxon bill or various indecency acts keep the Ameri-

can Civil Liberties Union, libertarian artists, and congress on their toes. New technologies in aggregate increase the (a) availability, (b) realism, (c) choice, and (d) extreme versions of obscene materials to children, psychotics, pedophiles, and public alike. Safeguards against accidental intrusion are available to parents, librarians, and so forth, but systems are not foolproof, free, or ubiquitous. Virtual reality, satellites, the internet, web, and multimedia all provide different problems, from the Playboy channel being accidentally beamed to Iraq, to 6-year-olds accidentally viewing sodomy online.

34. *Physiological damage:* Conflicting research and reports about whether cellular phone use is linked to brain tumors or more conclusive research that high exposure to computer monitors may be damaging to pregnant women alert companies, consumers, and lawyers alike to new domains of concern and litigation. Scientists such as Berger (1996) and journalists such as Giorgianni (1996) have reported some correlation between the use of headphones and permanent hearing loss. Perhaps a larger issue than known effects are the unknown effects, insufficient testing, and the Exxon Valdez effect, that is, concern catapults only after problems are publicized.

35. *Plagiarism:* Now that it is frequently less possible or impossible to determine authorship, the standards as to what constitutes plagiarism are in question. When lack of documentation (more frequent on the internet than in print) leads to accidental and incidental plagiarism, who is accountable? When hypertext links lead from author to author to anonymous data to transient site to pseudodocument, how can one be sure of (a) authenticity, (b) authorship, (c) original authorship, and (d) accuracy? Students now cite the internet as if it is an author itself. Such problems further complicate related issues of copyright, intellectual property, and ownership.

36. *Privacy:* Problems relating to privacy invasion, including surveillance, data theft and hijacking, impersonation to obtain information or records, unauthorized access, circulation of incorrect data, online voyeurism, wiretapping and taping, espionage, intrusion to telebanking, telemarketing, online campaign strategies, and so forth, are now among the largest for corporations, state agencies, institutions, and individuals to detect and counter. From the macrolevel of satellites to the microworld of minicameras and hidden hackers, snooping and scooping multiply. Remote sensing satellites, encryption breakers, and undetected data duplicators (invisible thieves) further compound new privacy problems (Cooper, 1995; CERT, 1995; Flaherty, 1984; Hausman, 1994; Ludlow, 1996).

37. *Satellite imagery:* Not only a specialized case of privacy and surveillance, satellite imagery involves also a complex thicket of legal issues about who the images belong to. Whether the press should have access to pic-

tures showing foreign military installations or whether entrepreneurs can sell images detecting hidden precious metal deposits to the highest bidder become debatable questions. To photograph someone from several miles high is not the same as to photograph him or her in a bathroom, but the hidden nature of the satellite that may also be in neutral, or foreign, or contended airspace further mixes issues of privacy, espionage, secrecy, ownership, transborder invasion, and voyeurism simultaneously.

38. *Security:* Closely linked with issues of privacy, piracy, counterfeiting, bootlegging, viruses, theft, encryption, and related problems, security has become a major parasite industry surrounding most new technologies. An insecure or leaky cellular phone system may lead to overheard conversations (such as have recently led to the publishing of Newt Gingrich's ethics violation phone calls or have led to a wife divorcing her husband due to overhearing his cellular conversation with his mistress). Video and audiotape duplication and the piracy of electronic information have become multibillion dollar industries worldwide. From one ethical perspective, it is immoral to be a pirate or thief, yet, from another, that features pirate's manifestos and other liberation documents, it is unethical to secure, encrypt, or own information that should be freely available in the first place. Subtechnologies and softwares featuring security become their own industries that, ironically, often only create a breed of craftier and more competitive thieves (Anonymous, 1996; Ludlow, 1996).

> The stress of being unable to keep up with information. . .

39. *Psychological damage:* Although difficult to detect, some mental problems associated with new technologies are commonly reported. Wurham's (1989) Information Anxiety that featured the stress of being unable to keep up with information overload (from innumerable faxes, e-mail, memos, teleconferences, cyberlists, software upgrades, constant on-the-job learning, and so forth) is widely experienced in institutional and corporate life. Meanwhile, excessive exposure to violent video games has been associated with trauma and anxiety among youngsters. Some TV cartoons have been suggested to possibly trigger epileptic seizures ("Television Cartoons," 1997), whereas the debate about how much violent behavior is catalyzed by technology icons and modeling continues. Questions about what happens to the collective psyche of an overloaded, noisy, image-laden, station-to-station (rather than person-to-person), wired-womb society are yet to be determined, although many critics note disturbing tendencies.

40. *Viruses:* Although the common perception of a virus is that it can attack or destroy computers, the megareality has evolved that viruses can

potentially destroy intelligent society by infecting entire systems, security agents, operations controls, and the defense networks of countries and companies. Viruses can infect with phony information, can transmit to other systems, can destroy immune systems, and sabotage or redirect military systems, and, when fully operant, deliver a knock-out punch to nerve centers as vital as Wall Street or nuclear monitoring systems. Although security technology such as SATAN (and new super SATANic) software is intended as a benign service to detect leaks in one's own systems, in the wrong hands such leak-busters become break-in path detectors for virus transmitters, thieves, and saboteurs. Rumors and myths about omniviruses, which could quickly destroy all online civilization, albeit inflated and overcirculated, have roots in breeding realities.

Types of Relations[2]

Although one could posit innumerable types of relations between new communication technologies and the effects and issues they accompany, this research suggests seven primary types. New technologies (a) amplify, (b) obsolesce, (c) create, (d) perpetuate, or (e) retrieve existing effects and ethical issues. In addition, the ethical issues and effects reveal (f) a mixture of the effects and issues or (g) the effects and issues are unknown.

To give simple examples, cable, satellites, and internet all amplify the problems of obscenity and indecency by making controversial and criminal (in many cultures) images available to much larger, different, and younger audiences. However, technologies of encryption, scrambling, and security (e.g., internet nannies and grannies) struggle to obsolesce such effects and issues within specific technologies, regions, and institutions.

Other technologies such as the computer terminal or cellular phone, respectively, can create new effects and issues such as radiation poisoning to pregnant operators or (possibly) brain tumors to consumers. Other technologies simply perpetuate or continue existing problems: Online newspapers perpetuate journalism's problems with the naming of rape victims or unnamed sources.

An interesting feature of some new technologies is that they retrieve or bring back new versions of old devices. The new telephone voicemail feature that allows department secretaries to leave spoken announcements on all office telephones retrieves the town crier or village messenger. Similarly, the computer virus brings back the *animal saboteur* from medieval days who smuggled animals with contagious diseases into the flocks of enemies.

When invasion of privacy occurs with old technologies such as a camera capturing a naked celebrity on the Riviera, such invasion has very different qualities than *cyvacy*, computer privacy invasion. In many instances, the latter is remote, undetectable, and global in scope—entire economies, electric systems, campaign strategies, transportation routings, missile destinations, and so forth can be altered. Privacy invasion is no longer personal but is transformed to global and impersonal.

Often, such relations between a technology are mixed (e.g., fiberoptics may attempt to obsolesce one problem but may in fact create another). Finally, many relations are unknown. Some research may suggest that televised violence inspires greater real-world violence; other research may infer that TV violence offers catharsis to a violent society; still, other research about the effects of TV violence are inconclusive. If the effects of televised violence remain debated and unknown after half a century, how may the effects of children's computer game ultraviolence be conclusively known after half a decade?

The New Factors

Researchers in the area of new technology ethics and effects will need to become even more humble than their predecessors. Several factors make a thorough understanding and comprehensive analysis of the field unique:

1. *Acceleration:* The rate of invention and implementation of new communication devices and software, together with their concomitant and unknown effects and issues, increases each year.

2. *Reactive atmosphere:* Ethics problems are usually only studied in depth after serious problems are created. A preventive rather than reactive atmosphere would allow some problems to be anticipated if not prevented.

3. *Invisibility:* Early, Sieber (1986) reported that most computer crime in Germany alone was undetected and much more unreported. It is difficult to study the effects and issues surrounding what is undetected and unreported.

4. *Multinational and multicultural problems:* Numerous new communication systems cross national boundaries without passports. Understanding cultures, languages, intercultural interaction, national laws, ethical mores, and policies becomes crucial.

5. *Combination effects:* Noted biochemist Ross Hume Hall (1974) discovered that food additives that test positive in isolation sometimes test negative or toxic when combined. Lack of research about the effects of new technologies is further compounded by the seeming total ignorance about the effects of new technology interaction. If each technology has possible or profound effects, what are the by-products of compound interactivity?

6. *Personal domain:* Professional ethics practices and violations are often in the spotlight and considered public domain research. However, when

the primary day-to-day violations become unauthorized tape duplication, software copying, and internet porn access, all behind closed doors, knowledge about widespread suburban and urban practices becomes all but off-limits to research. Much abuse is more manifestly covert or personal.

7. *Boundary blur:* Just as the boundaries between multimedia components become blurred, so do the boundaries of the ethical issues that surround them. Issues and effects link not-so-neatly one to another and pole vault into other dimensions and pages of context like hypertext linkage. Seeking to analyze the ethics of the internet becomes like nailing jello to the wall. The more shapes change, the more slipperiness remains the same.

These and many other challenges to research dictate that those employing, studying, and creating policy for new technologies will need to study the patterns surrounding the observation of new technology as much as the technologies themselves. As Innis (1951a, 1951b) noted, each new technology will also itself influence the way we think and engage. Thus, the very technologies we use to study and communicate technology influence our personal and cultural biases. Our new lenses must be taken into account when we attempt to "read" new social spectacles.

Recommendations

The question whether technology controls society or vice versa is a question of dominion. In Kohler's (1997) instructive case study about the way traditional media companies will employ new technologies, Dominion is well-founded as the company name. To dominate the technology, executives and researchers in companies like Dominion must study and understand potential long-range effects and ethical issues associated with their inventions. Otherwise, as companies like America Online have already demonstrated, problems inherent within the implementation of technology and problems inherent in forgetting to understand and study the human consequences of the new technologies will begin to dominate the company and society.

Hence, these recommendations follow, not only for executives at Dominion, a metaphor for all businessess seeking to implement new communication products and services, but also for ethicists, researchers, citizens, and students who seek to study new technology effects and ethical issues, whether in the lab, library, field, home, or classroom.

1. *Far greater presearch is needed.* Presearch occurs prior to the marketing, publicizing, and especially distributing of new technologies. Presearch involves testing technologies with test groups, comparing them with existing and similar tools to look for common and related issues and effects. Presearch welcomes cooperation with consumer groups, scientific experts,

government inspectors, and others to consider the possible consequences of new technology deployment.

2. *Independent thinking and reflection are essential.* The speed-up quality of the information age must be countered with deliberate periods of slow-down. Think tanks, conferences, retreats, silent periods, reflection memos, overview sessions, guest speakers, consultant sessions, and especially deliberate individual discipline regarding independent thought are crucial in corporate and institutional cultures overlaid with their own levels of intracommunication smotherage.

3. *Human and humane emphases are crucial.* When America Online emphasized growth over customer service, a signal was sent to customers that greed, not consumer relations, was the raison d'etre for their provider (an inaccurate descriptor). As researchers study the effects of technologies on human beings, they are not only acting within the interest of society's welfare but also within their own corporate interest by preventing law suits, low morale, customer dissatisfaction, and, thus, a lack of dominion.

4. *Depth analysis must penetrate well beyond the conventional wisdom.* Recently, a field representative for a major multinational company tried to sell new communication technologies in the Pacific. Pointing out how locals could receive help from medical information online, she said "these services will help you people combat disease." Regrettably, she had failed to perceive that it was the very people who brought new technologies into their culture years ago who had imported diseases in the first place. To the locals, the technology representatives and the technologies were themselves disease carriers. Similarly, journalists who have written scathing editorials about the destruction of forests and consequent depletion of oxygen are themselves adding to deforestation with the publication of massive, largely unread papers. Thought must be systemic, holistic, and multidisciplinary, taking viewers themselves and their context into account.

> **Problems inherent in forgetting to understand . . .**

5. *Ethicists, policy providers, legislators, and others must shift gears.* The notion that the internet, World Wide Web, and related phenomena are trends that will soon be passé has been widely held by scholars, corporate giants, and analysts who wish to stay in second gear. However, unless lawmakers, policy experts, governments, researchers, and ethicists—not to mention informed citizens—keep pace with entrepreneurs, inventors, and brush-fire products, profits and commercialism will soon replace social welfare and civic balance as national priorities.

6. *Tolerance of uncertainty and ambiguity.* Despite the human tendency to want closure, those studying new technologies must be especially patient, tolerant of ambiguity, and open-minded. Especially with new products, inventions, and services, conclusive research is not immediate and often conflicted and complex. Those researching and employing new technologies require greater flexibility and versatility. Too many factors, variables, and implements make conceptual closure about definitive effects and issues premature.

7. *Systematization.* Nevertheless, despite the need to stay open, some ability to perceive patterns and problems is crucial. Books such as Pavlik's (1998) *New Media Technology* are helpful in charting and organizing what is known about the new implements. Indeed, this essay is an attempt to list what is known about the related social conundra. Bibliographies, courses, workshops, conferences, websites, and published empirical research may further help reduce ignorance if not bring complete knowledge.

8. *Commit to Mann and Heidegger.* Immersed in a sea of challenges and often inhumane effects, the idealist is often summoned to follow the dictum commonly attributed to Horace Mann: "Be ashamed to die until you have won some fight for humanity." In this regard, there are now more windmills with which to tilt and more runaway technologies to corral. However, Heidegger's (1968) observation "that which is slipping away is thinking" (p. 17) rings equally loud. Sometimes, the acts of tilting and corralling do more harm than good and create more problems than they solve. If crusading, counterbalancing, and regulating are ever required, they must be equally tempered with education, studying, reflecting, and a wise balance between extremes.

Summary

The important Swiss scientist Hans Jenny (1967) noted in his study of *cymatics*—the science of vibration and oscillation—that ripples and structures respond to and are shaped by specific frequencies of sound and signal. If each technology is seen as carrying a new, signature oscillation or vibration within it, we will better understand how it ripples thoughout society causing both excitement and disturbance.

Understanding effects and ethical issues accompanying new technologies includes studying a myriad of overt and submerged social, cultural, and institutional factors within corporations and countries. Such understanding involves studying the cymatics or signature wavelengths of each technology and of the context (cultures, domains) within which it interacts.

To have dominion over such new technologies and to predict at least some of their effects, it is important to recognize, systematize, analyze, and tentatively evaluate not only technologies but their relations to corporations, individuals, and societies. Despite the great distance of that journey, this author wishes to begin it with this single step.

Notes

1. Like all attempts at structure, this list and analysis are incomplete and embryonic. Terms overlap, key words listed could be replaced by their synonyms, and identifying phrases and terms vary with the industry, academy, and society. Nevertheless, some categorical nomenclature is necessary. Moreover, this author has no objection to those who wish to modify, expand, and refine the following terminology. More important is the task of providing awareness of the immense scope of issues for media companies and students of communication. Indeed, a huge spectrum of issues exist that must be researched and discussed within the industry, the academy, and society. The following list and analysis are two of many catalysts toward such research and discussion. Although selective and ever-changing, this budding list is compiled from (a) many conferences, texts, tapes, seminars, websites, and publications about the new communications technologies; (b) first hand encounters; and (c) independent thinking. Although 40 is both arbitrary and delimiting, any number would be, and this number will grow in months to come. In the age of hypertext, it is not surprising that issues not only overlap but often lead one to another. Any list will always be incomplete, soon dated, culture-specific, and, thus, to some degree, subjective. A scholar, farmer, or executive who lives in a communist, Mennonite, Navaho, nudist, military, or Microsoft (corporate) community would view ethics in a different way and might even know of top secret technologies and other issues.

2. Notations of causation and technological determinism are extremely problematic (as in Ellul, 1964; Giedion, 1948, 1967; Innis, 1951a, 1951b; McLuhan, 1964; Mumford, 1956, 1962; White, 1962). A technology may not cause or be the full reason for what we call an effect or related ethics issue. The invention may simply cause a new corridor for ethical and unethical behavior or exist within an adjacent domain. There are often multiple and unknown catalysts stimulating many seeming and real effects and issues, and, with new technologies, it becomes all the more difficult to find long-term users, research, and, thus, patterns. There are even schools of thought that suggest that the notion of effects is illusory because forces that create the ripple also created the pond and the pebble; that is, large systems, whether historical, metaphysical, physical, Divine, or evolutionary, are at work creating local cause and effect illusions. Moreover, an effect is not identical to an ethical issue. Only when the two become so inextricably linked, as with new technologies, are they listed together as previously. One effect of the new technology—motion detecting satellites (that is, with more powerful long-distance cameras that automatically zoom in on motion)—might be more aerial espionage or surveillance worldwide. Such an effect (worldwide surveillance) quickly becomes an ethical issue when surveillance is perceived as invasion of privacy. Similar instances of bonded effects and ethics phenomena are dramatic and widespread.

References

Anonymous. (1996). So you want to be a pirate? In P. Ludlow (Ed.), *High noon on the electronic frontier* (pp. 109–112). Cambridge, MA: MIT Press.

Arnheim, R. (1971) *Film as art.* Los Angeles: University of California Press.

Bagdikian, B. (1997). *The media monopoly* (5th ed.). Boston: Beacon.

Barlow, J. (1996). Selling wine without bottles: The economy of mind on the global net. In P. Ludlow (Ed.), *High noon on the electronic frontier* (pp. 9–34). Cambridge, MA: MIT Press.

Berger, E. (1996, December 24). Say what? These headphones can be hazardous to hearing. *Hartford Courant*, p. B4.

CERT. (1995). *Cert advisory: Security administrator tool for analyzing networks (SA-TAN).* Pittsburgh, PA: Carnegie Mellon University.

Cooper, T. (1986–1987). Communication and ethics: The informal and formal curricula. *Journal of Mass Media Ethics, 2,* 71–79.

Cooper, T. (1995, December). Leading ethical issues concerning communication and privacy. *Pacific Telecommunications Review.* Honolulu, HI: University of Hawaii Press.

Cooper, T. (1997). *A time before deception: Truth in communication culture and ethics.* Santa Fe, NM: Clear Light.

Curtis, P. (1996). MUDing: Social phenomena in text-based virtual realities. In P. Ludlow (Ed.), *High noon on the electronic frontier: Conceptual issues in cyberspace* (pp. 347–374). Cambridge, MA: MIT Press.

Ellul, J. (1964). *The technological society.* New York: Vintage.

Ereira, A. (Director), & Mystic Fire Corp. (Producer). (1991). *From the heart of the world: The elder brother's warning* [Film]. (Available from BBC Enterprises Limited)

Flaherty, D. (1984). *Protecting privacy in two-way electronic services.* White Plains, NY: Knowledge Industry.

Garfinkel, S., Stallman, R., & Kapor, M. (1996). Why patents are bad for software. In P. Ludlow (Ed.), *High Noon on the electronic frontier: Conceptual issues in cyberspace* (pp. 35–62). Cambridge, MA: MIT Press.

Giedion, S. (1948). *Mechanization takes command.* New York: Oxford University Press.

Giedion, S. (1967). *Space, time, and architecture.* Cambridge, MA: Harvard University Press.

Giorgianni, A. (1996, December 24). Say what? Those headphones can be hazardous to hearing. *Hartford Courant*, p. B4.

Godwin, M. (1996). Some "property" problems in a computer crime prosecution. In P. Ludlow (Ed.), *High noon on the electronic frontier: Conceptual issues in cyberspace* (pp. 113–122). Cambridge, MA: MIT Press.

Hall, R. (1974). *Food for naught: Decline in nutrition.* Philadelphia: Lippincott.

Hausman, C. (1994). Information age ethics: Privacy ground rules for navigating in cyberspace. *Journal of Mass Media Ethics, 9,* 135–144.

Heckel, P. (1996). Debunking the software patent myths. In P. Ludlow (Ed.), *High noon on the electronic frontier: Conceptual issues in cyberspace* (pp. 63–108). Cambridge, MA: MIT Press.

Heidegger, M. (1968). *What is called thinking*. New York: Harper & Row.

Huxley, A. (1932). *Brave new world*. New York: Bantam.

Innis, H. (1951a). *The bias of communication*. Toronto, Canada: The University of Toronto Press.

Innis, H. (1951b). *Empire and communication*. Toronto, Canada: The University of Toronto Press.

Jenny, H. (1967). *Cymatics*. Basel, Switzerland: Basilium.

Kohler, P. (1997, February). *Caught in the web: The case of dominion media*. IRTS Foundation Faculty/Industry Seminar Case Study, New York.

Kubrick, S. (Producer & Director). (1968). *2001: A space odyssey* [Film]. (Available from MGM-UA Pictures)

Lamberton, D. (1997). Television down under. *Media Ethics, 9*, 21–22.

Ludlow, P. (Ed.). (1996). *High noon on the electronic frontier: Conceptual issues in cyberspace*. Cambridge, MA: MIT Press.

McLuhan, M. (1964). *Understanding media*. New York: McGraw Hill.

McLuhan, M. (1975, February 3). Culture and Technology Seminar, University of Toronto, Toronto, Ontario.

Mitroff, I., & Bennis, W. (1989). *The unreality industry and the deliberate manufacturing of falsehood: What it is doing to our lives*. New York: Oxford University Press.

Mumford, L. (1956). *The transformation of man*. New York: Harper & Row.

Mumford, L. (1962). *Technics and civilization*. New York: Harcourt, Brace, & World. (Original work published 1934)

Ogden, M. (1991). Preliminary report on the social impact of television in Palau and the Marshall Islands. In J. Savag & D. Wedemeyer (Eds.), *Pacific Telecommunications Council Thirteenth Annual Conference* (pp. 845–851). Honolulu, HI: Pacific Telecommunications Council.

Orwell, G. (1949). *1984*. New York: New American.

Pavlik, J. (1996, 1998). *New media technology: Cultural and commercial perspectives*. Needham Heights, MA: Simon & Schuster.

Powell, A. (1994). On ramps to the information superhighway. *Media Studies Journal, 3*, 113–121.

Postman, N. (1988). *Amusing ourselves to death: Public discourse in the age of show business*. New York: Penguin.

Schaeffer, M. (1977). *Tuning the earth*. New York: Harper & Row.

Shannon, C., & Weaver, W. (1949). *The mathematical theory of communications*. Urbana: University of Illinois Press.

Sieber, U. (1986). *The international handbook of computer crime*. New York: Wiley & Sons.

Singer, J. (1996). Virtual anonymity: Online accountability and the virtuous virtual journalist. *Journal of Mass Media Ethics, 12*, 95–106.

"Television cartoons send children into seizures in Japan." (1997, December 21) *New York Times*, p. 4:2.

White, L., Jr. (1962). *Medieval technology and social change*. New York: Oxford University Press.

Wurham, R. (1989). *Information anxiety*. New York: Doubleday.

Yap . . . How did you know we'd like TV? (1987). Directed by Dennis O'Rourke. Produced by O'Rourke Associates Los Angeles, Direct Cinema Limited.

Recommended Reading

Alter, J. (1990, July 30). When photographs lie. *Newsweek*, p. 44.

Black, J. (1994). *Aeropagitica* in the information age. *Journal of Mass Media Ethics, 9,* 131–134.

Bok, S. (1997). *Lying: Moral choice in public and private life* (6th ed.). New York: Pantheon.

Bruckman, A. (1996). Gender swapping on the internet. In P. Ludlow (Ed.), *High noon on the electronic frontier* (pp. 317–326). Cambridge, MA: MIT Press.

Champion, J. (1993). The commandments. *Compute!, 15,* 128.

Chong, R. (1993). Zap, crackle, and pop: Health concerns in the U.S. as to radio frequency electric and magnetic fields emitted from telecommunications facilities. In *Pacific Telecommunications Council Fifteenth Annual Conference* (pp. 150–156). Honolulu, Hawaii: Pacific Telecommunications Council.

Christians, C., Fackler, M., Rotzoll, K., & McKeet, K. (1998). *Media ethics: Cases and moral reasoning* (5th ed.). New York: Longman.

Collins, R., & Murroni, C. (1996). *New media, new policies: Media and communications strategies for the future.* Cambridge, England: Blackwell.

Cooper, T. (1993, Spring). Communication as corpus callosum. A reorganization of knowledge: Centrality of communications bridge between hemispheres. *Journalism Educator*, pp. 84–88.

Davis, D. (1993). Social impact of cellular telephone usage in Hawaii. In *Pacific Telecommunications Council Fifteenth Annual Conference* (pp. 641–648). Honolulu, Hawaii: Pacific Telecommunications Council.

Denning, D., & Barlow, J. (1996). The Denning-Barlow clipper chip debate. In P. Ludlow (Ed.), *High noon on the electronic frontier: Conceptual issues in cyberspace* (pp. 215–216). Cambridge, MA: MIT Press.

Digiovanna, J. (1996). Losing your voice on the internet. In P. Ludlow (Ed.), *High noon on the electronic frontier: Conceptual issues in cyberspace* (pp. 445–458). Cambridge, MA: MIT Press.

Dizard, W. (1997). *Old media/new media: Mass Communications in the information age.* New York: Longman.

Dominick, J., Sherman, B., & Copeland, G. (1990). *Broadcasting/cable and beyond: An intro to modern electronic media.* New York: McGraw Hill.

Dunlak, J. (1991). Hype and reality in interactive media. In *Pacific Telecommunications Council Thirteenth Annual Conference* (pp. 450–455). Honolulu, Hawaii: Pacific Telecommunications.

Elmer-Dewitt, P. (1996). Censoring cyberspace. In P. Ludlow (Ed.), *High noon on the electronic frontier: Conceptual issues in cyberspace* (pp. 259–262). Cambridge, MA: MIT Press.

Forester, T., & Morrison, P. (1993). *Computer ethics: Cautionary tales and ethical dilemmas in computing* (2nd ed.). Cambridge, MA: MIT Press.

Freedman, B. (1994, May 30). Computing ethics. *PC Week*, p. 123.

Gladney, G. (1994). Bringing communication technology under ethical analysis: A case study of newspaper audiotex. *Journal of Mass Media Ethics, 9*, 243–257.

Glazier, S. (1993). Software, patents, ownership, and infringement crimes: New developments. In *Pacific Telecommunications Council Fifteenth Annual Conference* (pp. 922–928). Honolulu, Hawaii: Pacific Telecommunications Council.

Gotterbard, D. (1991, Summer). Computer ethics. *National Forum*, pp. 26–32.

Gross, L. (1986). *The new TV technologies*. Dubuque, IA: Brown.

Heinberg, R. (1979). *Resonance*. Toronto, Canada: Read/Lee.

Hodges, L. (1994). The journalist and privacy. *Journal of Mass Media Ethics, 9*, 197–212.

Husselbee, J. (1994). Respecting privacy in an information society: A journalist's dilemma. *Journal of Mass Media Ethics, 9*, 145–156.

Johnson, D. (1991, Summer). Computers and ethics. *National Forum*, pp. 15–18.

Koch, T. (1991). *Journalism in the 21st century: Online information, electronic databases, and the news*. London: Adamantine.

Levinson, P. (1988). *Mind at large: Knowing in the technological age*. Greenwich, CT: JAI.

Mace, S. (1994, July 4). Campaign puts focus on ethics in computing. *Infoworld*, pp. 16, 17.

Makau, J., & Arnett, R. (1996). *Communication ethics in an age of diversity*. Urbana: University of Illinois Press.

Mercedes, D. (1996, May). Digital ethics: Computers, photographs, and the manipulation of the pixels. *Art Education*, pp. 44–51.

Milton, B. (1993). Managing the privacy implications of new technology. In *Pacific Telecommunications Council Fifteenth Annual Conference* (pp. 929–933). Honolulu, HI: Pacific Telecommunications Council.

Mitcham, C. (1996, March). Technology and ethics. *World and I*, pp. 314–329.

National Institute of Standards and Technology. (1995). *SATAN Software rollfact sheet*. Washington, DC: NIST.

Noll, A. (1996). *Highway of dreams: A critical view along the information superhighway*. Mahwah, NJ: Lawrence Erlbaum Associates, Inc.

Organization for Economic Cooperation and Development. (1981). *Guidelines on the protection of privacy and transborder flows of personal data*. Paris: OECD.

Orlik, P. (1992). *The electronic media*. Needham, MA: Allyn & Bacon.

Poole, B. (1994, September). Cybertrespassing. *Compute!*, p. 120.

Powell, A. (1994, April 6). *Speech, Technology Studies Seminar*. New York: Freedom Forum Media Studies Center.

Powell, A. (1994, October 27). *Speech, Technology Studies Seminar*. New York: Freedom Forum Media Studies Center.

Rahim, S., & Wedemeyer, D. (Eds.). (1983). *Telecom Pacific*. Honolulu, Hawaii: Pacific Telecommunications Council.

Reeves, B. (1996). *The media equation: How people treat computers, television, and new media as real people and places*. Cambridge, England: Cambridge University Press.

Salton, G. (1980). A progress report on information privacy and data security. *Journal of the American Society for Information Science, 31*, 75–83.

Simpson, R. (1995, September 8). Choices and the feel-right factor. *Times Higher Education Supplement*, p. 6.

Smith, R. (1993). *Our vanishing privacy*. Port Townsend, WA: Loompanics Unlimited.

Spector, P. (1993). Wireless communications and personal freedom. In *Pacific Telecommunications Council Fifteenth Annual Conference* (pp. 250–252). Honolulu, Hawaii: Pacific Telecommunications Council.

Tenner, E. (1991, November/December). The impending information implosion. *Hantard Magazine*, pp. 24–27.

Turkle, S. (1996). *Life on the screen*. New York: Simon & Schuster.

Vislosky, D. (1994, May). Ethics and computers. *Byte*, pp. 41–43.

Watson-Gegeo, K., & White, G. (Eds.). (1990). *Disentangling: Conflict discourse in Pacific societies*. Stanford, CA: Stanford University Press.

White, P. (1993). Caller ID and privacy: New options. In *Pacific Telecommunications Council Fifteenth Annual Conference* (pp. 917–921). Honolulu, Hawaii: Pacific Telecommunications Council.

Williams, F. (1992). *The new communications* (3rd ed.). Belmont, CA: Wadsworth.

Woo, J. (1993). The personal data protection regime emerging in Korea. In *Pacific Telecommunications Council Fifteenth Annual Conference* (pp. 934–941). Honolulu, Hawaii: Pacific Telecommunications Council.

Journal of Mass Media Ethics
Volume 13, Number 2, pp. 93–98

Satellite Imagery: The Ethics of a New Technology

By Adam Clayton Powell, III
The Freedom Forum (New York)

❏*In the bygone days of U-2 spy planes and Sputnik, the only ethical issues attached to satellites seemed to involve military secrecy and national boundaries. Now, with high-powered lenses, infrared sensory devices, ubiquitous satellites, and instant high-resolution image transmission, the communication ethics issues—like the powers of global observation—have greatly magnified. Possibly, conventional warfare has become obsolete because television networks have access to 9 worldwide satellite images that show troops, fleets, and fighter squadrons forming prior to attack. Civilian privacy has changed drastically as well because backyard sunbathers, naturalists, couples, speeding vehicles, and naked paramours seen through bedroom windows can all be identified, photographed, and publicized without their awareness or permission. Because the power, range, frequency, and commercialism of such space photography will increase, ethicists must survey the surveillance. Vendors in many countries now routinely sell space imagery to news outlets. This means there are at least two types of communication ethics to consider: (a) In journalism ethics, editors and producers must decide whether they will publish many types of invasive photographs, some of which may also deal with military secrecy; and (b) in new media ethics, decisions about who employs, duplicates, regulates, as well as who sells and buys satellite imagery, must be monitored and debated.*

In the bygone age of U-2 spy planes and Sputnik, the ethical issues attached to satellites involved military secrecy and national boundaries. With high-powered lenses, infrared sensory devices, ubiquitous satellites, and instant high-resolution image transmission, the communication ethics issues, like the powers of global observation, have greatly magnified.

Possibly, conventional warfare has become obsolete because television networks have access to worldwide satellite images that show troops, fleets, and fighter squadrons forming prior to attack. Civilian privacy has changed drastically as well because backyard sunbathers, naturalists, couples, speeding vehicles, and naked paramours seen through bedroom windows can all be identified, photographed, and publicized without their awareness or permission.

Because the power, range, frequency, and commercialism of such space photography will increase, ethicists must survey the surveillance. Vendors in many countries now routinely sell space imagery to news outlets. This means there are at least two types of communication ethics to consider: (a) In journalism ethics, editors and producers must decide whether they will publish many types of invasive photographs, some of which may also deal with military secrecy; and (b) in new media ethics, decisions about who employs, duplicates, regulates, as well as who sells and buys satellite imagery, must be the subject of discussion.

When Sputnik, the world's first artificial earth satellite, went into orbit in 1957, fears of surveillance from the skies sent military planners into an orbit of their own. For years, U.S. reconnaissance aircraft had flown high over the Soviet Union and Eastern Europe, snapping highly detailed photographs of army formations, naval bases, and other military information.

However, the American public was at best vaguely aware of these missions, only occasionally reminded during the Cuban missile crisis or when a U-2 spy plane was shot down over Russia.

Sputnik permitted Russians to introduce surveillance of the United States and Western Europe by collecting photographs of American army formations and naval bases. Although the first Sputnik could do little more than send beeping signals, ranking officials knew that the first satellite would soon be followed by others that would send detailed photo images, not just beeps.

On hearing first word of Sputnik's launch, one senior American general sputtered, "Those bastards!" (Stuhlinger, 1997). Within months, Sputnik 1 was followed by Sputnik 2, and then, after a crash program, the United States launched the first American satellite, Explorer 1, in early 1958. A succession of orbiting platforms for photographic reconnaissance followed, some spacecraft weighing tons and capable of sending first radio transmissions of photo images and later dropping small capsules of exposed film back into the atmosphere for recovery by intelligence agencies.

After spending $100 billion on the U.S. program (Graham, 1996) and another considerable sum in Russia, the owners of the technology could produce a level of photographic detail so great that officials boasted of being able to read license plates in the parking lot of the Soviet naval base in Vladivostok. So many of these programs were secret that their histories have yet to be published.

Historians agree that these orbiting platforms have been useful in preventing wars between the super powers because space-based imagery has provided a routine method of checking on adversaries. Although bad weather can interfere with some observations, unless military installations are buried deep under ground or otherwise hidden from view, orbiting satellites can keep track of them with ease.

We can glean a hint of still-classified satellite capabilities from informed fiction, such as the depiction of visual and infrared sensors in the movie *Patriot Games* (Neufeld, Rehme, & Noyce, 1992). Even more dramatic was the capability demonstrated in the report on the Trans World Airlines 747 crash off Long Island in the video produced by the Central Intelligence Agency. The CIA is barred by law from spying on Americans, but one of its satellites just happened to be looking at Long Island at the moment the TWA jet exploded.

Until recently, the ethics of space-based imagery was a subject of little interest outside of the occasional science-fiction writer's dream of a distant future when all of us might have access to pictures from space, no doubt watching them in our personal flying automobiles. However, the future is now. We do not have personal flying automobiles; however, the dream of widespread distribution of pictures from space is a reality. The privatization of America's espionage technology is delivering *Patriot Games* reconnaissance imagery to corporations and newsrooms at a very affordable price.

The cozy superpower duopoly began to collapse when the French entered the space reconnaissance business and began to treat it as a business by selling satellite images. The French still sell images to governments, and the Bosnia peace accords are monitored in part by commercial images from France's SPOT Image Corporation (Satellite images, 1996). Another early client was *ABC News*. Mark Brender (1993), ABC's defense producer, realized such imagery could revolutionize television news and quickly began buying images of places that had forbidden ABC camera crews. *World News Tonight* began showing pictures of secret military installations in North Korea, weapons plants deep inside Iran, and mysterious laboratories in the Russian heartland.

These were not conventional aerial photographs: By combining SPOT Image digital photos taken from varied angles, computers could reconstruct three-dimensional depictions (just as the human brain constructs a 3-D world from the images of our two eyes). Once the depiction was calculated, computers could construct television displays of a scene that let a producer show "fly-throughs," as if the viewer were on an airplane flying slowly and at low altitude over the formerly hidden site.

Early SPOT images were expensive, but, after SPOT, space-based imagery became a business, and SPOT soon had competitors. The Russians, eager for hard currency transactions, began to offer their top-secret satellite imagery for sale. They already had their assets in orbit and wished to maximize their revenue.

Now, U.S. companies, concerned that they are losing the commercial space race, are entering the field. High-resolution images are now available to local governments, farm agencies, and newsrooms at an affordable price. The *Miami Herald* used satellite imagery to demonstrate discriminatory housing patterns in southern Florida. Already, image vendors are setting up booths at journalism conferences to show reporters and editors how they can catch polluters or cover forest fires with 3-D "fly-throughs" from space.

Brender (1997) said he believes satellite imagery will be the end of conventional warfare because news organizations will be able to spot preparations for attacks anywhere in the world. He claims every army in the world can be seen, including troop formations and airplanes.

For example, during the Gulf War, anyone with access to satellite imagery would have seen the U.S. troops moving through the desert for their surprise attack on Iraqi forces. Despite requests from ABC News and others, SPOT Image declined to sell images of Iraq to any of its clients, amid reports the United States suggested it might disable the SPOT cameras with lasers if they tried to televise the battle. Moreover, Israel has been able to obtain agreements that vendors may not sell images of its defensive positions to news organizations—or to anyone else. Just because satellites can observe from the skies does not mean the end of military censorship, at least by the big powers.

Early journalistic uses of space images have been for reporting war and the threat of war. Yet, today's noble purposes will become tomorrow's staple. In 1998, vendors promise, everyone will be able to dial up high-resolution images on the World Wide Web. Just as thousands subscribe to the *Wall Street Journal* online, anyone with a credit card will be able to go to one of the competing sites and order high-resolution images, which will be delivered via e-mail to one's computer.

Editors are beginning to worry that the issues of war and peace will soon be supplanted by seamier applications of space-based imaging for tabloid photos—and worse. "If we were any other group, we'd be worried about the media using it," said Kenneth E. Bildermback, manager of the New Media Group for the *Columbian* (Vancouver, WA) at a June 1996 satellite imagery conference at the Freedom Forum Pacific Coast Center. Andrew Voros, editor of the *Manteca* (CA) *Bulletin*, agreed that cheap satellite pictures are great tools for editors, "but the door for abuse is wide open" (Freedom Forum, 1996).

As editors recognize the capabilities of the new satellite services, they realize they themselves will be under observation. "We all want to catch pimps and prostitutes, but I drove 85 miles an hour to get here," said Rusty Coates, online manager for the *Sacramento Bee*, "and I sure as hell don't want someone watching me" (Freedom Forum, 1996).

As with so many new technologies, the issues raised are as old as journalism, or older. In this case, the issue is the line between reporting a legitimate news story and voyeurism. "If you can see in a back yard without standing on a ladder, it's legitimate," observed photographer Bill Knowland of Direct Images. "But if you stand on a ladder and start shooting, that's something else. Now you're up in a satellite" (Freedom Forum, 1996).

In addition, from a satellite, every backyard, every rooftop, and, if the light is good, every window is an opportunity for the invasion of privacy. As long as we were tiny dots in an aerial photograph, anonymity was intact. However, now, with high-resolution satellites, we can see individual humans—us—photographed from cameras gliding silently in orbit miles overhead. "What would be an unreasonable breach of your privacy?" asks Knowland. "Are we talking about one person filling the entire screen?"

These are not theoretical questions. The government of San Francisco commissioned detailed aerial images of the entire city to help produce more accurate maps. Some news organizations demanded access to the photographs early this year under Freedom of Information provisions. Nonetheless, there was a problem: The images were so detailed that individuals in their back yards and on the decks could be seen, where they presumed no one was watching. Nude sunbathing was the least offensive of various R- and X-rated activities.

Using new civilian versions of military reconnaissance technology, television news helicopters hovering at considerable distance can now transmit live close-up broadcast-quality pictures of breaking news—or anything else. Indeed, the newest equipment now enables television stations—or anyone else—to stand or hover at a great distance and transmit live pictures of news at night, merging visual and infrared sensors to generate a detailed live picture after dark of breaking nighttime news—or of unlimited other possibilities. Using thermal imagery, nighttime darkness and even solid objects are no longer barriers to news coverage.

"It cuts through smoke and also things like leaves," said a clearly delighted Bill Carey, news director of WCBS-TV in New York (Dickson, 1997). Introduced in February 1997, over 50 of these devices had been delivered to television stations by October (Proctor, 1997). Television viewers can watch crimes in progress in the dark of night. "Patriot Games" has come to the 11 o'clock news and to the tabloids..

British television may be best known to U.S. viewers for Masterpiece Theater and Jane Austen. Yet, one of the best-selling British videos of all time was *Caught in the Act*, a compilation gathered by security cameras in offices, stores, and parking lots. Intended to fight crime, the cameras silently observed everything taking place.

The images of interest to the producers of *Caught in the Act* were exactly those acts that people commit when they assume no one is watching. Suffice it to say the video will not be shown soon on broadcast television.

Caught in the Act was hugely profitable, and, if the British follow the Hollywood model, they will soon begin production of *Caught in the Act – Part 2*. This time, instead of security cameras, they will scan high-resolution images from space, looking at back yards, rooftops, and beaches around the world. *Mondo Cane* meets *Candid Camera*, all rated X.

Satellite vendors may not be eager to fill an order from the *Caught in the Act* production team. However, the images are already on file: The producers need not produce any new videos. In the course of reporting on war and peace, famine, and floods, satellite images already show the entire range of human activity, in color and 3-D. The city of San Francisco has documented everything that was taking place outdoors on the sunny day its mapping photos were taken. Satellite images of that secret Russian arms plant showed everything taking place outdoors in the area. In high resolution, we are all *Caught in the Act*.

What we mean by invasion of privacy is *Caught in the Act* of changing in scope, distance, and magnitude. If war may change to peace due to the monitoring of troops, peace may change to war due to the monitoring of private citizens. Ultimately, ethicists inherit a much more wide angle field for their steady surveillance.

References

Brender, M. (1993, February). *The technological and legal implications of journalists' use of satellite imagery.* Technology Seminar, Freedom Forum Media Studies Center, New York.

Brender, M. (1997, May 31). Lecture, The Newseum, Arlington, VA.

Dickson, G. (1997, October 20). WCBS–TV cuts through Gotham gloom. *Broadcasting & Cable, 127*(43), 62.

Freedom Forum Pacific Coast Center Conference on Satellite Imagery. (1996, June).

Graham, M. (1996, July). High resolution, unresolved. *Atlantic Monthly, pp.* 24–28.

Neufeld, M., & Rehme, R. (Producers), & Noyce, P. (Director). (1992). *Patriot Games* [Film]. (Available from Paramount Pictures)

Proctor, P. (1997). Industry outlook: Film at 11. *Aviation Week & Space Technology, 147*(15), 13.

Satellite images. (1996, Spring–Summer). *SPOTlight,* p.1.

Stuhlinger, E. (1997, October 4). *Sputnik 40 years later: Science, the news media and the Future.* Speech given at the Freedom Forum, Arlington, VA.

Journal of Mass Media Ethics
Volume 13, Number 2, pp. 99–110

Plain Reservations: Amish and Mennonite Views of Media and Computers

By Donald B. Kraybill
Messiah College

❏*Five ethical objections to the use of mass media and the internet help explain why the Plain People of North America avoid new communication technologies. Each subgroup of plain folk—including Amish, Mennonites, and Brethren—adopt differing amounts of new technology, and the use varies from region to region or even from community to community. Old media such as the radio and telephone and newer media such as television and the internet introduce different and unwelcome moral values into plain communities, although the telephone is often a borderline case. The ethical systems of the Old Order groups provide a unique and pragmatic critique of the widespread acceptance of mass media and the internet in the larger social world.*

The Plain People of North America worry that mass media and the internet will ruin their souls and lead to the demolition of their communities. Old Order Amish and Mennonite groups have consistently banned access to many forms of media, old and new, in the hopes of preserving their collective soul. Drawing lines in the social sand between themselves and the larger society, these groups believe that the values purveyed by the new communication technologies will contaminate their culture and lead to its demise. Who are these groups, what do they value, and why are they so anxious about mass media?

Who Are the Plain People?

Present day Mennonites and Amish trace their lineage to the Anabaptists of 16th-century Europe. The Anabaptists emerged in 1525 in southern Germany and Switzerland in the wake of the Protestant Reformation. Members of the new "free" church movement were called Anabaptists (rebaptizers) because they insisted on baptizing adults based on a voluntary confession of faith. Known as radical reformers, many Anabaptists paid dearly for tearing asunder the fabric of church-state ties that had been woven so tightly over the centuries. Thousands were tortured and killed by religious and civil authorities —burned at the stake, drowned in lakes and rivers, starved in prisons, and beheaded by the sword.

Descendants of the Anabaptists migrated to North America in the 18th and 19th centuries in search of religious freedom and fertile land. Today, they are clustered in some 50 subgroups and number about 525,000 in the United States (Hostetter, 1997). Many Anabaptist groups have blended into modern culture. The Old Order Anabaptist communities highlighted in this article number about 200,000; these groups have actively resisted acculturation and assimilation.[1]

Old Order Mennonites. Mennonites take their name from a prominent church leader, Menno Simons, who converted from Catholicism to Anabaptism in 1536. Swiss and South-German Mennonite immigrants settled in Pennsylvania throughout the 18th century and became known for their expertise as farmers. Today, members of acculturated Mennonite groups accept higher education, employ modern technology, participate in professional occupations, dress in contemporary styles, use mass media and produce radio and television programs—typically for religious purposes.

Old Order Mennonites, by contrast, frown on higher education, place restrictions on technology, and typically embrace a more rural and conservative lifestyle. The Old Orders can be sorted into two major types—those who drive motor vehicles and those who continue to use horse-drawn transportation. This article focuses on the more conservative groups—the horse-and-buggy Mennonites—who separated from more progressive Mennonites in the late 19th century.

Old Order Amish. Amish prominence in the national consciousness has spiraled since mid century with the rise of tourism and generous media coverage. Today, millions of tourists visit Amish communities each year. The feature film *Witness* (Feldman & Weir, 1985) scattered Amish images on theater screens around the world, and the music video parody "Amish Paradise" by Weird Al Yankovic enjoyed heavy rotation on MTV in the spring of 1996.[2] *Vogue* magazine recently featured 14 color pages of trends in "plain" clothing worn by models framed by a variety of Amish props—buggies, hay bales, and horse-drawn machinery. Computer buffs can even buy an "Amish" software program that, of course, has nothing to do with the Amish. These and many other examples attest to the ways in which the Amish have become objects of public curiosity.

The Amish story began in 1693 when Swiss and South German Anabaptists divided into two religious streams: Amish and Mennonite. Jakob Ammann, an Anabaptist elder, sought to revitalize the church in several ways. Social and theological differences as well as personal entanglements led to a permanent division. Ammann's followers were eventually called Amish.

Although they all share a common history from 1525 until 1693, the Amish and Mennonites have maintained separate identities since the 1693 division. Although the Amish often find themselves in the public spotlight, they prefer to live quiet, undisturbed lives. They live alongside their English-speaking neighbors in small villages and farming communities in more than 250 settlements in 23 states.

The Mennonites and Amish share some practices but differ on others. Both groups use horse and buggy transportation, speak the Pennsylvania German Dialect, wear plain dress, end formal schooling at the eighth grade and hold strict taboos on television, radios, VCRs, and computers.

Several differences separate the two groups. The Amish worship in their homes, meeting every other week for a 3-hour service. The Mennonites worship in austere meeting houses that seat 300 to 500 people but do not have electricity or modern heating. Unlike the horse-farming Amish, the Mennonites use tractors with steel wheels to pull machinery on their fields.

The Mennonites tap 110-volt electricity from public utility lines and have telephones in their homes, whereas the Amish do not. Apart from these and other minor differences, the Amish and Mennonites subscribe to common Old Order values and appear fairly similar to the outside world.

Separation from the World

Old Order groups are what sociologists sometimes call sectarian groups because they draw sharp lines of separation between themselves and the larger society. Mainstream cultural values are viewed as a threat to their religious faith and practice. Separation from the world is based on biblical phrases such as "Be not conformed to the world, Love not the world or the things of the world," "Come out from among them and be ye separate saith the Lord," and "Be not unequally yoked together with unbelievers." The outside world in the sectarian mind denotes the larger social system with its unregenerate values, vices, and practices. Separation from the world is maintained by specific practices as well as special symbols. These cultural fences remind insiders and outsiders alike of the borders between the sectarian enclave and the dominant culture.

A variety of symbols articulate nonconformity in Old Order communities. The horse and carriage used by Mennonites and Amish symbolize their rejection of the larger culture. These groups also require their members to wear distinctive garb which signals separation from the world and compliance with community rules. These symbols are ethnic flags that announce sectarian loyalties and mark the boundaries of ethnic turf. The principle of nonconformity regulates the rate of social change, the use of technology, as well as leisure activities that intersect with the larger society.

The culture of Old Order groups rests on the bedrock of *Gelassenheit*—a German word that roughly means yielding and surrendering to a higher authority. However, Gelassenheit is layered with many meanings—self surrender and self denial, resignation to God's will, yielding to others, gentleness, a calm and contented spirit, and a quiet acceptance of whatever comes. Although the word rarely is spoken, the meaning of Gelassenheit is woven into the social fabric of Old Order life. It reflects the most fundamental difference between Old Order culture and modern values (Kraybill, 1989).

The ways of Gelassenheit are difficult to comprehend in a world saturated with personal ambition and padded resumés. Whereas modern culture heralds individual achievement, advancement, and personal recognition, Gelassenheit calls for hesitating, slowing down, and backing off. The modern focus on individual rights and personal ambition flies in the face of Gelassenheit. In a community regulated by the virtues of Gelassenheit, the collectivity—not the individual—is the primary social unit.

Members are urged not to boast or do things that call attention to themselves. Pleas for humility and simplicity remind members that, as Christians, they are called to self-denial and obedience to the church. The discipline of the Mennonite church says, "Let us be plain and humble in our homes, clothing, carriages, and everything we own."

Selective Use of Technology

The restrictions these groups have placed on the mass media and the internet rest on their principles of separation from the world. The media by their very nature provide access to the values of contemporary culture. More than providing access, the media funnel the latest images, sounds, and ideas directly into the homes of those who are wired for them. Such access to mass media technology poses a serious threat to Old Order communities. They fear that exposure to modern values will spoil not only their religious beliefs but their total way of life. By barricading themselves off from media sources, the Plain People believe that they can insulate themselves from evil forces that might otherwise contaminate their cultural values. The Amish taboo on 110-volt electricity from public utility lines, established in the early part of the 20th century, has essentially eliminated their access to the mass media.[3]

The Plain People are not modern day Luddites who disparage new technology. They do, however, selectively screen new forms of technology to determine their potential harm to the community. New technology that enhances economic and agricultural productivity is widely accepted if it fits or can be adapted to the guidelines of Amish culture.[4] For example, state-of-the-art hay balers designed to be pulled and powered by tractors are purchased from English farm machinery dealers. Amish tradition dictates that farmers use horses to pull farm machinery.

Imaginative Amish mechanics have learned to retrofit the balers by installing gasoline engines on them so they can be pulled by horses. Some communities have recently adopted rollerblade skates and gas barbeque grills without making any modifications to them. Battery operated, handheld calculators have long been used by farmers and businessmen.

In broad terms, the Old Order response to technology is threefold. They will (a) accept new forms of technology that are considered helpful benign to the welfare of the community, (b) adopt new technology that can be adapted to fit the regulations of the community, and (c) reject technology that will likely be detrimental to the community.

New modes of technology that are directly related to agriculture or commercial production have been widely accepted. More restrictions and taboos have been placed on communication technology than on any other type. Because influences from the larger world pose a major threat to Old Order communities, communication technologies are carefully screened.

The filtering of new technology is largely informal. Innovators within the community may start using a form of technology such as a hand-held calculator to test the reaction of church leaders. If the innovation does not provoke too much resistance and if it is not considered dangerous to the well-being of the community, it will gradually be adopted into Old Order culture. Church leaders never formally accept or officially bless a new gadget; it is welcomed instead by benign neglect and implicit sanction.

Church leaders may arrest the introduction of a "dangerous" technology immediately or require it to be adapted to traditional standards of Amish or Mennonite practice. In the mid 1980s, a few members of the Amish community purchased computers and operated them in clandestine sites in barns or small manufacturing shops. In most cases, the computers were powered by batteries.

As the presence of computers became public knowledge in the community, church leaders worried that their use would lead to television, which has been an uncontested taboo in the community for many years. Because the monitors for personal computers look much like television screens, Old Order leaders thought the computers would open the door to television. Moreover, stories were afloat in the community about mischievous youths playing video games on personal computers. Worried that computers would lead to television and open the door to the outside world, church leaders in the late 1980s banned the ownership of computers.

The discussion swirling around computers led to an important accommodation, however, for business owners who needed word processing equipment. Church leaders agreed to a compromise: Word processors with a small display screen would be permitted. This handy compromise enabled proprietors to conduct their necessary business while, at the same time, allaying the fears of church leaders about computers.[5] Using small word processors at home was considered quite a different matter than tapping into television.

Ethical Objections to Electronic Media

Separation from the world is the explicit reason that Old Order leaders give for rejecting the use of computers, internet, television, and radio. These communication media threaten the moral order of the plain communities in at least five different ways.

First, the individualistic values that saturate media programming directly challenge the communal nature of Old Order life. To have their members drink at the trough of individualism would, over time, erode the very foundation of their culture. The images and content of contemporary film and television purvey unchallenged assumptions about individual rights, freedom, choice, and options, all of which directly contradict Old Order understandings of obedience, submission, and self denial.

Second, the secular nature of modern media also challenges Old Order life. Although not expressing their religious faith in a loud and noisy fashion, a spiritual world view does undergird their total cultural system. In many ways, their religious views are founded on traditional understandings rather than on a formal system of theology. The secular and relativistic worldview that dominates mass media would completely upend the root values and worldview of Old Order life.

A third objection focuses on sexuality and family values. Nudity, sexual relations outside of marriage, divorce, and homosexuality are unacceptable options in Old Order life. They are simply viewed as sin—as moral infractions that will lead to eternal damnation. Old Order people believe that such "immoral" behavior is forbidden by scripture, and practitioners should be excommunicated from the church.

Media programs that favorably accept what Old Order people consider degenerate family values challenge their entire social system that is anchored on the traditional extended family. Modesty, purity, and life-long commitments to marriage are unquestioned virtues. To expose members to opposing values is not only foolish but dangerous as well.

A fourth objection involves the force and violence that permeate television and film. As conscientious objectors, the Plain People eschew the use of force even for self-defense. Based on Jesus's admonition to love one's enemy, they categorically reject violence as incompatible with Christian faith. A member who joins the military or who files a lawsuit will be excommunicated because the people believe that such use of force violates God's will for the human community. Consequently, they contend that their members should completely avoid any forms of media that accept, or even worse, endorse the use of violence.

Finally, a fifth objection concerns a multitude of modern values that are antithetical to their way of life. Many of the underlying values that shape the content of mass media contradict Old Order understandings of the good life. The Plain People emphasize hard work, frugality, and simplicity. They frown on materialism, commercialized leisure, gambling, and amusement. If such activities—reflecting the heart throb of modern culture—would fill screens and monitors in Old Order homes they would gradually demolish the bedrock values of their society.

An Amish guide for living renders harsh judgment on the media.

> Few of us have heard anything through the news media that added one inch to our stature or helped us to be better men and women in this life. If we have read the sickening details of one war, rape, robbery, murder, riot or famine . . . . what shall it profit us if we hear of a thousand more. (*1001 Questions*, 1992, pp. 142–143)

To the Old Order mind, these objectionable features of the mass media make it patently clear that it would be foolish and tantamount to social suicide to permit their members to plug into electronic media. The modern media are considered a menace that must be kept at bay lest they contaminate the minds of the faithful and lead to the demise of their community.

Communication Technologies

As Table 1 shows, technology that provides direct access to the outside world creates the most concern and is typically forbidden. Television, radio, and the internet are simply off the cultural screen because they offer immediate and unfiltered access.

Television stirs little discussion because it clearly violates the moral order of the community. In the words of one Old Order member, "television is the sewer line that connects you directly to the cesspool of Hollywood." Radio and television, according to an Amish guide are

> forms of worldly entertainment . . . . How many minds have been damaged and polluted by the diet of romance and violence from these media? Forsaking these is one of the first and most important steps for anyone. (*1001 Questions*, 1992, p. 142)

The rejected communicative tools—television, CD players, and VCRs—are typically one-way devices that permit outside influence but cannot be used for internal communication. An exception to this is the CB radio, which

Table 1. Old Order Usage of Communication Technologies

Acceptance	Adaptive	Rejection
Hand-held calculators	Telephone	Television
Desktop calculators	Fax machine	Computer
Word processors	Answering machines	Internet
	Beepers	Radio
		Tape recorders
		VCRs
		CD players
		CB radios

could, like the telephone, facilitate both internal and external use. Demand for CB radio has never surfaced, therefore the CB has not come into use. Church leaders would have likely rejected the CB radio for fear it would lead to the use of standard radios.

Telephones have provoked more controversy in Old Order communities than any other form of technology.[6] The ambiguity of the telephone rested on the fact that it could serve the ethnic community for internal communication as well as tie the community to the outside world. The telephone has enjoyed a cantankerous history within Old Order communities. In the first decade of the 20th century, both Amish and Mennonite churches forbade its use. A few families who had installed telephones were subsequently asked to remove them when the church placed a taboo on the phone. A direct line to the outside world was a clear and obvious violation of separation from the world. Moreover, face-to-face communication, with all the rich accessories of body language and ethnic costume, was the primary source of social solidarity within the community. "Visiting" was, in the words of one Amish man, "our national sport." The telephone not only welcomed strangers, it also threatened to reduce face-to-face communication. Why visit if you can call?

Given these concerns, the church leaders banned telephones in the first decade of the 20th century. However, they did not forbid the use of them altogether. Members could use a telephone in an English neighbor's home or in a public setting. In both contexts, an Old Order member was using a phone to place outgoing calls to care for an emergency, to call a veterinarian, or to make an appointment with a doctor or dentist. Strangers could not initiate calls to members unless they had established a prearranged time.

As the 20th century unfolded, church members persistently pleaded for greater access to phones. Some English neighbors were annoyed by the growing number of requests from manure-smelling farmers to use the phones in their kitchens. In dense settlements, Old Order farms stretched for miles, making it inconvenient to find a phone in a neighbor's home or a public place to call a veterinarian. Consequently, Mennonite resistance to the telephone waned by midcentury. Mennonite leaders eventually permitted phones to be installed in homes and shops. For several years, ministers were not permitted to install them—a continuing sign of the church's discomfort. By the 1980s, however, the telephone was well ensconced in Mennonite homes.

The telephone received a cooler reception among the Amish. By midcentury, church officials had agreed to the use of "community telephones" placed at the end of farm lanes. These phone shanties, looking much like an outhouse, were shared by several families to make outgoing calls. This development defined an intriguing tie with technology. Telephones, at the end of the lane, would serve the community, despite some inconvenience, when members needed access to the outside world. However, the telephone would not dominate, control, or alter the basic rhythm of Amish life. It was technology in service of the community but clearly and cautiously held at bay.

The telephone shanties have inched ever closer to homes, barns, and shops in the last two decades. Today the Old Order Amish continue to prohibit the installation of telephones in their homes. The local bishop has the freedom to determine the location of telephones in his church district of some 30 households. In some progressive districts telephones are installed inside barns and shops, while at most homesteads they remain outside the shop or at the end of the lane. Commercial interests have clearly drawn them closer to barn and shop where they are used regularly.

The "understandings" or tacit agreements about media technology are taken seriously in Old Order communities. These understandings are incorporated into the *Ordnung*—the body of rules and regulations that prescribe expected behavior among the Plain People. Functioning as a policy manual of sorts, the unwritten Ordnung is transmitted orally across the generations by word and deed. Young children informally absorb the ways of Old Order life as they grow up in the community. Young adults are typically baptized between the ages of 18 and 22. Upon baptism, they promise to uphold the norms of the Ordnung for the rest of their lives. Those who renege on their baptismal pledge face excommunication and shunning if they are unwilling to repent and confess their wrongdoing.

A baptized adult who purchases a television or a computer will receive a visit by church officials and be asked to "put the item away," that is, sell it. If the deviant complies he or she will be restored into membership with a mild rebuke. Should offenders refuse to abandon the illegitimate item they are subsequently excommunicated and subject to social ostracism until they are willing to confess their ways. Depending on the circumstances, they may remain outside the fold for the rest of their lives.

The teenage years provide a curious exception—a zone of freedom from church restrictions. Young people typically begin dating and "running around" at the age of 16. Because the plain groups practice endogamy, youth must be baptized prior to marriage. This liminal period, roughly stretching from age 16 to about age 21, offers a band of freedom. No longer closely supervised by their parents nor yet under the jurisdictional thumb of the church, youth sometimes experiment with the outside world.

Some youth groups are rather docile and enjoy their freedom within the boundaries of Amish life. The more rebellious ones cast off their Amish garb and flirt with the way of the world. A few young men purchase automobiles and have free access to radios. Other enterprising youth may continue to use horse and buggy but may install a radio or CD player in their buggy. Rebellious teens sometimes own televisions, and it is not uncommon for them to view Hollywood films in local theatres. Upwards of 85% will eventually join the church and, upon baptism, they will "put away" their worldly toys and settle into the mature routines of adult Amish life. A young male with a radio or CD player in his buggy will tear it out prior to baptism and marriage.

Thus, although most Old Order adults do not have regular access to communication technologies, some of them have had exposure to such devices in their prebaptism years.

Cultural Compromises

Some intriguing riddles of Old Order life arise from the cultural compromises that these groups have struck while struggling to maintain their ethnic identity in the face of burgeoning technological developments. At first blush, these adaptations appear silly to outsiders—riding in motor vehicles but not owning them, accepting 12-volt electricity from batteries but not the 110-volt variety from public utility lines, and placing phones at the end of farm lanes but not in their homes. The Old Order groups informally negotiated with modernity, and the resulting cultural compromises took several forms: (a) a distinction between the use and ownership of technology, (b) mechanical adaptations of certain types of technology, and (c) restrictions governing the use of technology.

These interesting compromises, in a variety of ways, permitted the churches to regulate the use of technology, control its impact on the community, and limit individual access. The distinction between use and ownership of autos allowed members to use taxi service provided by their English neighbors. This service boosted the economic productivity of small shops that desperately needed motor vehicles to transport supplies and products while preserving horse-drawn transportation for family purposes.

Likewise, with the telephone, individuals were free to use phones in the home of a neighbor or in public places—an arrangement that enhanced the economic well-being of the community. By keeping phones out of homes and regulating their use and placement, the Amish were able to control their impact and remind members of their potential danger.

A variety of other compromises have emerged as well. Amish construction crews traveling to work sites in vans owned and operated by English neighbors are permitted to listen to the radio in the van on a daily basis. Old Order folks traveling in rented vans to an out-of-state wedding or funeral will also listen to a radio. If travelers stay in a motel overnight, they will often watch television. Amish persons who work as domestics in private homes or who work in motels or restaurants will also watch some television as well. In all these instances, the community draws a sharp line between use and ownership of the technology. The occasional use of a radio or television owned by someone else serves as a social immunization, so to speak, that confirms in Old Order minds how much trash is indeed on the air waves.

A similar distinction relates to the use of the computer, but, in this case, commercial interests have encouraged the compromise. Some Old Order people work for English employers, and, in an occupational setting, they are permitted to use computers. Amish business people will sometimes lease a computer or contract with an outside vendor for computer services for payroll and inventory management. Such arrangements are typically acceptable to the church so long as they do not lead to mischief and eventual ownership.

Some Mennonite farmers have a weather radio—a single band monitor that permits them to hear occasional weather reports for farming purposes. These are frowned on by church leaders for fear they will lead to full-fledged radios. One Mennonite community only permits black phones and not more than one phone and one extension per family. Cordless phones, fax machines, answering machines, and any other "unnecessary" accessories are off limits in this particular settlement.

All these unusual arrangements are compromises of one sort or another that enable these ethnic communities to preserve their Old Order identity while tapping the benefits of technological progress. Certain that direct exposure to mass media and the internet will contaminate their cherished values and undermine their way of life, they are nevertheless willing to make some adaptations that enable them to prosper economically. In so doing, they are able to maintain their viability as a distinctive subculture in American society.

Notes

1. See an introduction to Amish life and culture in Kraybill (1989). Scott (1996) provides an overview of Old Order Mennonite groups.
2. The taboo of Old Order communities on Hollywood feature films in theatres and television was one of the reasons the Amish objected so strenuously to the filming of the feature film *Witness*. The Amish attitude toward *Witness* is told by Hostetler and Kraybill (1988).
3. The problems posed by electricity for Old Order communities is described by Scott and Pellman (1990).
4. The Amish struggle with technological innovation in the context of modern society is addressed in Kraybill and Olshan (1994).
5. Compromises with technology prompted by commercial activities are detailed by Kraybill and Nolt (1995).
6. The story of the Amish struggle with the telephone is told by Kraybill (1989) and Umble (1996).

References

Feldman, E. (Producer), & Weir, P. (Director). (1985). *Witness* [Film]. (Available from Paramount Pictures U.S.A.)

Hostetler, J., & Kraybill, D. (1988). Hollywood markets the Amish. In L. Gross, J. Katz, & J. Ruby (Eds.), *Image ethics: The moral rights of subjects in photographs, film, and television* (pp. 220–235). New York: Oxford University Press.

Hostetter, C. (1997). *Anabaptist-Mennonites nationwide USA*. Morgantown, PA: Masthof.

Kraybill, D. (1989). *The riddle of Amish culture*. Baltimore: The Johns Hopkins University Press.

Kraybill, D., & Nolt, S. (1995). *Amish enterprise: From plows to profits*. Baltimore: The Johns Hopkins University Press.

Kraybill, D., & Olshan, M. (1994). *The Amish struggle with modernity*. Hanover, NH: University Press of New England.

1001 questions and answers on the Christian life. (1992). Aylmer, Canada: Pathway.

Scott, S. (1996). *An introduction to Old Order and conservative Mennonite groups*. Intercourse, PA: Good Books.

Scott, S., & Pellman, K. (1990). *Living without electricity*. Intercourse, PA: Good Books.

Umble, D. (1996). *Holding the line: The telephone in Old Order Mennonite and Amish life*. Baltimore: The Johns Hopkins University Press.

Journal of Mass Media Ethics
Volume 13, Number 2, pp. 111–123

Virtually Transcendent: Cyberculture and the Body

By David J. Gunkel[1]
Northern Illinois University

❏This article examines the ethical implications of the desire for disembodiment situated in the texts and technologies of cyberspace. The article is divided into 2 parts. The first traces the conceptual history of dualism, demonstrating its exclusionary cultural politics and investigating the socio-political consequences of encoding this metaphysical information in contemporary media technology. The second part examines the material conditions of new communication technology, arguing that the issue of access reduplicates in practice the exclusivity of dualism. The article concludes by investigating the ethical implications of employing dualistic metaphysics as a legitimizing narrative of media technology and cyberculture.

For Case, who'd lived for the bodiless exultation of cyberspace, it was the Fall. In bars he'd frequented as a cowboy hotshot, the elite stance involved a certain relaxed contempt for the flesh. The body was meat. (Gibson, 1984, p. 6)

A recent MCI commercial (MCI, 1997) provided a succinct articulation of what has been considered the general ethos of the internet. "There is no race. There are no genders. There is no age. There are no infirmities." In this popular vision of cyberspace, the internet was presented as the great cultural mediator, leveling the differences that have divided and segregated human beings. The rationale animating this utopian promise lies in the technology's apparent disembodiment.[2] Cyberspace, it has been argued, provides a platform in which "people communicate mind to mind" (MCI, 1997) without the problematic constraints imposed by the meat-interface of differentiated bodies. As Dery (1994) explained in the introduction to *Flame Wars*, "The upside of incorporeal interaction [is] a technologically enabled, postmulticultural vision of identity disengaged from gender, ethnicity, and other problematic constructions. Online, users can float free of biological and sociocultural determinants" (pp. 2–3).

From the beginning, telemetric technologies have been informed by prophetic tales that forecast a time when we will be able to connect our consciousness to the matrix and surpass the cumbersome "meat" (Gibson, 1984, p. 6) of the body. This corporeal transcendence, which amounts to "nothing less than the desire to free the mind from the 'prison' of the body" (Biocca, Kim, & Levy, 1995, p. 7), not only constitutes one of the controlling ideals of cyberspatial systems (cf. Biocca et al., 1995; Gibson, 1984; Hillis, 1996; Interrogate the Internet, 1996) but comprises the essence of the age of information. "The central event of the 20th century," stated the Magna Carta for the Knowledge Age, "is the overthrow of matter. In technology, economics, and the politics of nations, wealth—in the form of physical resources—has been losing value and significance. The powers of mind are everywhere ascendant over the brute force of things" (Dyson, Gilder, Keyworth, & Toffler, 1996, p. 295). Heaven's Gate cult (1997) both worked on the internet and engaged in ascetic practices that not only denigrated the flesh (celibacy, castration, and so forth) but ultimately sought "to leave the containers of the bodies" is not a mere coincidence but symptomatic transcendentalism in the circuits of cyberculture.

This essay undertakes a critical examination of cyberculture's "transcendentalist fantasy" (Dery, 1996, p. 8). In particular, it investigates the ethics of this proclivity to be liberated from the meat of the body. This inquiry is oriented by two suspicions concerning the value of technology and the logic of emancipation.

First, as Penny (1994) has suggested, "all technologies are products of culture" (p. 234). Technology, therefore, is never neutral but always inflected and influenced by specific ideologies and preconceptions. The transcendental pretensions of cyberculture have been informed and substantiated by the conceptual divisibility of the mind from its body. This ideology, which is called dualism, is associated with specific sociocultural circumstances and has its own complicated history and ethical consequences. Employing dualism as a legitimating discourse, therefore, not only entails a specific metaphysical doctrine but incorporates all the social, political, and cultural implications that have been associated with it.

Second, emancipation is never a simple operation. As Hegel (1830/1987) pointed out in the *Encyclopedia of the Philosophical Sciences*, "the one who merely flees is not yet free; in fleeing he is still conditioned by that from which he flees" (p. 138). Liberation, therefore, is not a matter of mere flight or simple leave taking. The very means of release are often bound up with the mechanisms and systematics of domination. Emancipation from the body, therefore, may itself be materially conditioned, rendering corporeal transcendence far more complicated and entangled than it initially appears.

Despisers of the Body

In promising to facilitate bodily transcendence, the Internet participates in a larger project that constitutes one of the defining elements of the modern ethos. The obvious point of intersection, and the one most often mobilized in the discourse of cyberculture, is Descartes's *Meditations* (1641/ 1988)—said to have instituted not only modern philosophy but the doctrine of dualism. Dualism, the radical dissociation of the mind, or soul (Descartes conflated the two terms; cf. note 3, p. 74), from the body, does not, however, begin with Descartes. In Plato's (trans. 1961) *Cratylus* (circa 400), for example, Socrates suggested that the word "body" [σωμα] was coined by the Orphic poets who considered the living soul [ψυχη] to be incarcerated in the body as in a prison or grave [σημα]. This Orphic position is subsequently incorporated into the Platonic corpus in the *Phaedo* (Plato, trans. 1990), which is subtitled "On the Soul."

> We see the Internet as an expression of, and even the savior of high modernism. . . . It, above all else, promises the possibility of achieving the ends of the Enlightenment: a sense of mastery and escape from the limits of the frailties of incarnation. (Interrogate the Internet, 1996, p. 125)

According to tradition, the *Phaedo* not only argues for the separability of the soul from the body but provides several "proofs" for the soul's immortality (cf. Loraux, trans. 1989). Similar dualistic formulations are developed in Aristotle's (trans. 1907) *De Anima*, the Letters of St. Paul, the works of the Medieval neoplatonists (Plotinus, Augustine, and so forth), and the tradition of Scholasticism.[3]

The mind–body dichotomy, however, is not unique. Rather, this binary opposition participates in a general dualism that has constituted the very fabric of Western metaphysics. Metaphysics, which is not one region of knowledge among others but that on which such distinctions have been founded, is animated and informed by a network of dualities. "The fundamental faith of the metaphysicians," wrote Nietzsche (1886/1966), "is the faith in opposite values" (p. 2). A sampling of these opposite values that have been persistent in the Western tradition has been collected by Haraway (1991). They include, among others, "self/other, mind/body, culture/nature, male/female, civilized/primitive, reality/appearance, whole/part, agent/resource, maker/made, active/passive, right/wrong, truth/illusion, totality/partiality" (p. 177). Within the traditions of the West, these dualities are never situations of peaceful coexistence. Rather, they constitute violent hierarchies (Derrida, 1972/1981). As Elizabeth Grosz has explained (1994), "Dichotomous thinking necessarily hierarchizes and ranks the two polarized terms so that one becomes the privileged term and the other its suppressed, subordinated, negative counterpart" (p. 3). Within the Western tradition, mind has always been situated above and has ruled over the body, which has consequently been understood as the negation of everything that is determined of and for the mind. This determination, in turn, has been accomplished by mobilizing the elements of the other binary pairs that constitute the field of metaphysics. Mind, for example, is associated with divinity, whereas the body is relegated to the realm of brute animality. Mind is determined to be immortal; the body is perishable. Mind is whole or indivisible, whereas the body remains divisible. Mind is essential, the body merely accidental. Because of this precedence and privilege granted the mind over its negative and deficient other, Nietzsche (1892/ 1983) has characterized the general ethos of Western thought as "despisers of the body" (p. 146). The internet and its promised emancipation from the body, therefore, is nothing other than a technological incorporation of this ancient practice.

Discourses that promise liberation from the body through technology mobilize this tradition. The mind is posited as the essence of the person and is considered to be the source of one's true identity. The body and its complex of variations, on the contrary, is construed as a mere accident of biology, something that is inessential to what the individual actually is. Tracing the implications of this assumption, Gurak (1997) wrote:

> It is almost as if we could simply plug a coaxial cable directly into another person's brain and get at their true self, avoiding the messiness of race, gender, and other of these darn confounding variables that get in the way of who we truly are. (p. 1)

According to this logic, differentiation in gender, race, physical ability, and age are considered to be mere externalities that do not affect or belong to one's essential being. This formulation is not only consistent with the metaphysical understanding of difference as variations in and of the same (cf. Bataille, trans. 1985) but has traditionally been deployed to substantiate antisexist and antiracist positions. Elizabeth Spelman (1988) provided a rather succinct formulation of this procedure:

> Since the body, or at least certain of its aspects may be thought to be the culprit, the solution may seem to be: Keep the person and leave the occasion for oppression behind. Keep the woman, somehow, but leave behind the woman's body; keep the Black person but leave the blackness behind. (p. 128)

This formula for emancipation does not challenge the dualisms that structure Western thought but employs its despising of the body as the means by which to secure liberation from sexist and racist prejudice. Such a procedure, however, is doubly problematic. First, as Gurak (1997) argued:

To imagine that a technology, any technology, could possibly allow us to separate our minds from our social and emotional states encourages the worst kind of Cartesian thinking and detracts from our responsibility to learn how to live together in a diverse, complex democracy. It is dangerous to believe that you can escape into a space where issues of race and gender do not exist. (p. 2)

Second, and more fundamental, the doctrine of dualism does not challenge but has been the primary mechanism of prejudice and inequality. According to Leder (1990),

In our cultural hermeneutics women have consistently been associated with the bodily sphere. They have been linked with nature, sexuality, and the passions, whereas men have been identified with the rational mind. This equation implicitly legitimizes structures of domination. Just as the mind is superior to and should rule the body, so men, it is suggested, should rule over women. (p. 154)

Similar associations have been made in the area of race and ethnicity:

Certain kinds, or races, of people have been held to be more body-like than others, and this has meant that they are perceived as more animal-like and less god-like. For example, in the *White Man's Burden*, Winthrop Jordan (1974) describes ways in which white Englishmen portrayed black Africans as beastly, dirty, highly sexual beings. Lillian Smith (1961) tells us in *Killers of the Dream* how closely run together were her lessons about evil of the body and the evil of Blacks. (Spelman, 1988, p. 127)

Throughout the Western tradition, therefore, mind has been associated with and has served to legitimate specific positions of cultural hegemony. Dualism, then, is not merely an abstract formula. It is also a social and political principle that has substantiated and legitimated all kinds of prejudicial and exclusionary practices. Because of their associations with the body, certain persons and groups of people have been excluded from the transcendental domain of the mind.

Employing dualism as a legitimating narrative of liberation and equality, therefore, is necessarily complicated by these associations. Such discourses promise liberation from sexist and racist prejudice by deploying a concept that reinscribes and reinforces the very ideology of sexism and racism from which one would be liberated. This procedure is not only self-contradictory but insidious. It is contradictory insofar as it employs as a mechanism of social equality a dualistic formula that always and already excludes and marginalizes certain persons and groups of people. It is insidious, for it reinscribes traditional modes of domination and prejudice under the guise of liberation and equality. Under the discursive formulations circulated in the advertising of MCI, the fiction of cyberpunk, and the scholarly investigations like those initiated by Mark Dery (1996), Frank Biocca (Biocca et al., 1995), and Ken Hillis (1996), the internet has come to participate in these problematic operations. Through the rather naive formulations posed in these texts, telemetric technologies come to substantiate and reinforce the very systems of oppression and prejudice they promise to supersede and surpass. What is needed in assessing the sociocultural significance of the internet, therefore, is not a blind faith in the emancipatory and egalitarian rhetoric of technology but a critical engagement with the philosophical and cultural traditions that have come to empower and inform our employment and understanding of technological innovations. As Judith Butler (1990) suggested, "any uncritical reproduction of the mind/body distinction ought to be rethought for the implicit gender [and racial] hierarchy that the distinction has conventionally produced, maintained, and rationalized" (p. 12).

The Matter of Cyberspace

The doctrine of dualism is not a mere abstract ideology. It is also a practical mechanism of actual social and political discrimination. By employing this doctrine as a legitimating discourse, cyberculture necessarily comes to participate in this activity. As a result, individuals customarily associated with the body and materiality are restricted from participating in the incorporeal realm of cyberspace. This conceptual marginalization, however, does not remain at a mere ideological level. Rather, it is substantiated by the actual milieu of the internet. The net, therefore, not only reiterates current systems of domination through its employment of the doctrine of dualism but reinforces this discrimination in practice. To participate in cyberculture, one needs, minimally, a computer, modem, telephone service, and an internet service provider (ISP). One's access to the transcendent, virtual realm, therefore, is materially conditioned. In addition, it should be no surprise that those individuals generally restricted from accessing cyberspace are precisely those who have been traditionally marginalized because of their associations with the material of the body: women, people of color, and the impoverished.[4] Transcending the body, therefore, is a luxury that

> No network connection at all makes you a digital hermit, an outcast from cyberspace. The Net creates new opportunities, but exclusion from it becomes a new form of marginalization. (Mitchell, 1995, p. 18)

belongs to a certain group of people for whom material limitations in general have not traditionally been an issue. In this way, "the Net is not only another way to divide the world into haves and have nots" (Critical Art Ensemble [CAE], 1997, p. 6), but this information apartheid actually adheres to and reinforces current systems of oppression and inequality.

Cyberspace has been and remains the domain of white males. In this matter, John Perry Barlow, cofounder of the Electronic Frontier Foundation, did not realize with what exactitude he had described the evolving demographics of cyberspace: "Cyberspace . . . is presently inhabited almost exclusively by mountain men, desperadoes, and vigilantes, kind of a rough bunch" (Gans & Sirius, 1991, p. 49). Recent studies on computer usage and internet access corroborate this conclusion. According to a 1996 RAND report on computers and connectivity, the majority of U.S. "netizens" are male (68%), white (87%), college educated (64%), and highly compensated ($60,000 average annual income). This report not only found great discrepancies in access to cyberspace due to race, gender, and class but, by comparing the data obtained in 1996 with that from earlier studies conducted in 1993 and 1989, concluded that the gap between the information have and have nots has been growing steadily (Bikson & Paris, 1996).[5]

It should be noted, however, that this demographic information concerns internet usage in the United States. Global statistics, although currently unavailable, will obviously be more dramatic and potentially more disturbing, especially when one considers the fact that a majority the world's population does not have access to basic telephone service, "and hence it seems very unlikely that they will get a computer, let alone go on-line" (CAE, 1997, p. 6). From a global perspective, cyberspace remains a luxury of the postindustrial First World and, as a result, it is necessarily hardwired into the complications and paradoxes of colonialism (cf. CAE, 1997; Gunkel & Gunkel, 1997). Not only has the internet been considered "just another misunderstood 'white-man-thing'" (Dyrkton, 1996, p. 55), but experiments with telemetric technologies in the Third World have failed to provide the postcolonial liberation that has been espoused in the rhetoric of cyberculture theorists and multinational telecos like MCI. Rather, computer-mediated communication systems have actually reinforced current social inequities and systems of oppression. In June 1991, for example, the Organization of American States embarked on a plan to provide e-mail service to Caribbean and Latin American universities. Surveying the results of the SIRIAC (Integrated Informatic Resource System for Latin America and the Caribbean) program, Dyrkton (1996) made the following assessment:

> E-mail represents a significant advance for the university as a place on the margin of the Third World but it is also a political tool in a very polarized,

hierarchical society. E-mail can only exacerbate the gulf between classes; while it may help to rationalize the telephone system at various locations, it will not help realize appropriate sanitary facilities. The financially comfortable will learn to speak with computer literacy while the poor will continue in their world apart, just next door. (p. 56)

The question of technological access reinforces the complications encountered in the consideration of dualism. The internet has been determined to provide liberation from the problematic constraints of the body, namely, race, gender, and class. Access to this emancipation, however, is precisely dependent on one's race, gender, and class. Bodily transcendence via the internet, therefore, is a luxury that has been granted a group of individuals for whom race, gender, and class have never been problematic or restrictive. As Spinelli (1996) reminded us,

> The internet is not some kind of *deus ex machina* of democracy .... The Net is only an emergent medium, existing in a specific context with a real set of material confines, and possibly with a real potential. But it is a potential that will remain unrealized if we allow the drive to virtualize to obscure its material base and economic realities of our culture. (p. 14)

For this reason, women and people of color find themselves doubly excluded by the transcendentalist pretensions of cyberculture. They are not only always and already positioned outside the realm of mind through conceptual associations with materiality and the body but have been practically limited in their access to technologies that would promise to facilitate this transcendence.

Conclusion

From the beginning, cyberculture has been informed and directed by transcendentalist pretensions. Cyberspace, it has been suggested, not only liberates one from the meat of the body but, in doing so, promises to surpass sociocultural restrictions that have been the source of prejudice, exclusion, inequality, and domination. The eschatology of this transcendentalist thinking is nothing short of utopia—a global community emancipated from the problematic constraints of race, gender, age, infirmity, and so forth. This incorporeal exaltation, however, is not only informed by the ideology of dualism, which has its own complicated history and consequences, but remains a luxury that

> We have no reason to delude ourselves that any new technology, as such, promises any sort of sociocultural liberation. (Penny, 1994, p. 247)

belongs to a particular position of cultural hegemony. As Stone (1993) has recalled,

> Forgetting about the body is an old Cartesian trick, one that has unpleasant consequences for those bodies whose speech is silenced by the act of our forgetting; that is to say, those upon whose labor the act of forgetting the body is founded—usually women and minorities. (p. 113)

It is precisely through the transcendence of the meat, or data-trash (Kroker & Weinstein, 1994), of the body that Western thought has instituted and accomplished a violent erasure of other bodies and the body of the other.[6] Therefore, the cyberspatial researchers and critics who forecast and celebrate a utopian community in which "there is no race, there are no genders, there is no age, there are no infirmities" do so at the expense of those others who are always already excluded from participating in this magnificent, disembodied "technocracy" precisely because of their race, gender, age, class, and so forth. Far from resolving social inequities, this conceptualization of cyberspace perpetuates and reinforces current systems of privilege and domination, reinscribing traditional forms of mastery behind the facade of emancipation. In the end, what these various discourses *want to articulate* is resisted and undermined by what they are *compelled to articulate* because of the very metaphysical information they have deployed and utilized.

This dehiscence not only opens structural difficulties within the networks of cyberculture but, perhaps more importantly, implies rather disturbing ethical consequences. On the one hand, for those for whom material conditions have not been problematic, this transcendental rhetoric serves to obscure and to disguise current systems of privilege and oppression. In locating sociocultural emancipation in the transcendental promises of cyberspace, one not only promotes a mode of liberation that does not in any way problematize or question current positions of cultural privilege but obscures the fact that the very means of liberation is itself identical to the mechanisms of oppression. For the privileged few, these emancipatory promises bolster current modes of sovereignty while maintaining the facade of equity and democratization. On the other hand, for those already excluded through their association with materiality and the body, these emancipatory promises reinscribe current systems of domination. This procedure is not only contradictory but effectively legitimizes traditional forms of oppression and prejudice under the sign of emancipation. Unfortunately, this operation has all too often been the experience of those who have lived with and under oppression. Namely, what is promoted as liberation amounts to little more than another form of subjugation.

Notes

1. A nascent version of this text was presented at the second annual Ethics and Technology Conference at Loyola University, Chicago, June 1997.
2. For a brief analysis of the utopian rhetoric employed by MCI, cf. Gurak (1997).
3. Direct correspondence between cyberculture and the Judaeo-Christian tradition has been demonstrated in the texts of William Gibson. In an August 1993 interview on National Public Radio, Gibson explained that Neuromancer was based, in a large part, on "some ideas I'd gotten from reading D. H. Lawrence about the dichotomy of mind and body in Judaeo-Christian culture" (Dery, 1996, p. 248). As Dery (1996) explained by way of Meyers (1990), Lawrence had blamed St. Paul for his "emphasis on the division of the body and spirit, and his belief that the flesh is the source of corruption" (p. 236).
4. A good portion of the rhetoric surrounding the social significance of the internet comprises a digitalization of arguments that had been initially developed for earlier forms of communication technology, that is, printing, telegraph, radio, and television. One explanation for the apparent blind optimism and rather uncritical assessment of the internet is that we have simply forgotten, either deliberately or not, the lessons of history. Similar utopian rhetoric, for example, had been deployed with the emergent technology of wireless and radio broadcasting. In response to the FCC's antitrust investigations of RCA chief David Sarnoff espoused, in terms that explicitly foreshadow the MCI advertisement, the social benefits of broadcast communication. The importance of broadcasting cannot be measured in dollars and cents.

    > It must be appraised by the effects it has upon the daily lives of the people of America—not only the masses who constitute a listening audience numbered in the tens of millions, but the sick, the isolated, and the underprivileged, to whom radio is a boon beyond price. (Spinelli, 1996, p. 4)

    Commenting on the context of Sarnoff's speech, Martin Spinelli reminded us that this "utopian rhetoric . . . functioned largely to obscure a profit motive" (p. 8). The same maneuvers are evident within the texture of the MCI campaign. The social benefits ascribed to online communication serve not only to recode but simultaneously to conceal a specific motive for profit. From the perspective of a telecommunications corporation, race, gender, age, and infirmity are indeed irrelevant and inconsequential. For MCI, the race, gender, age, and health of its customers is accidental and superfluous. Telecommunications, unlike other commodities and services, is not restricted to a particular ethnic group, gender, or age. All that matters from the corporate perspective is that individuals become and remain consumers of services. It is under the recoded identity of consumer, therefore, that the MCI advertisement promises to erase difference and achieve social equality. For multinational telecommunications corporations, there is no race, there are no genders, there is no age, there are no infirmities; there are only consumers.

    It must be admitted that this operation is not unique in the world of advertising. Most commercials, whether in print or electronic media, function by associating a product with an intangible and desirable property, that is, love, success, freedom, social justice, and so forth (cf. Jacobson & Mazur, 1995). MCI, therefore, would seem to be in compliance with industry practice, engaging in what can only be called smart marketing. This approach, however, is rather devious and potentially dangerous. First, the advertisement promotes emancipation from oppression through subordination to a multinational teleco. This procedure suggests, ostensibly, resolving one form of subjugation by simply replacing it with another. Apart from the obvious structural contradiction, this stratagem is further complicated by the fact that one does not name this alternative subordination as such but bestows on it the contrary designation "liberation."

Second, through MCI's commodification of liberation, race, gender, and age are not so much transcended as they are translated and recoded. In the discourse of pancapitalism, this recoding always takes place in terms of class. It is no surprise, therefore, that class has been suspiciously absent from the advertisement's litany of emancipation. This programmed absence, however, is no mere accident. Excluded from the emancipatory potential offered by MCI will be those who cannot afford to be consumers of telecommunication technology. This includes individuals who do not have either the money for the apparatus, skill to use computers and telemetric systems, or both—statistically, women, people of color, and the aged. MCI, therefore, does not so much resolve the contemporary crises associated with race, gender, and age but recodes and redistributes these complications as class. Liberation from the problematic limitations of the body, therefore, is a luxury available only to those who can afford it; specifically those for whom corporeal limitations have not traditionally been restrictive or oppressive.

5. Similar results have been obtained in the Times Mirror national survey of 1994 and the 1995 Georgia Tech/Hermes survey of Web usage (Bikson & Paris, 1996; Hoffman, Novak, & Chatterjee, 1996).

6. For a critical examination of the fundamental exclusivity of Cartesian metaphysics, see Chang (1996).

References

Aristotle. (1907). *De Anima*. (R. Hicks, Trans.). Cambridge, MA: University Press.

Bataille, G. (1985). The use value of D. A. F. de Sade: An open letter to my current comrades (A. Stoekl, C. Lovitt, & D. Leslie, Trans.). In A. Stoekl (Ed.), *Visions of excess: Selected writings 1927–1939* (pp. 91–102). Minneapolis: University of Minnesota Press.

Biocca, F., Kim, T., & Levy, M. (1995). The vision of virtual reality. In F. Biocca & M. Levy (Eds.), *Communication in the age of virtual reality* (pp. 3–14). Hillsdale, NJ: Lawrence Erlbaum Associates, Inc.

Bikson, T., & Paris, C. (1996). Computers and connectivity: Current trends. Retrieved April 9, 1997 from the World Wide Web: http://www.rand.org/publication/MR/MR650/index.html

Butler, J. (1990). *Gender trouble: Feminism and the subversion of identity*. New York: Routledge.

Chang, B. (1996). *Deconstructing communication: Representation, subject, and econo-mies of exchange.* Minneapolis: University of Minnesota Press.

Critical Art Ensemble. (1997). Utopian promises—Net realities. Retrieved April 9, 1997 from the World Wide Web: http://www.well.com/user/hlr/texts/utopiancrit.html

Derrida, J. (1981). *Positions* (A. Bass, Trans.). Chicago: University of Chicago Press. (Original work published 1972)

Dery, M. (1994). Flame wars. In M. Dery (Ed.), *Flame wars: The discourse of cyberculture* (pp. 1–6). Durham, NC: Duke University Press.

Dery, M. (1996). *Escape velocity: Cyberculture at the end of the century.* New York: Grove.

Descartes, R. (1988). Meditations on first philosophy. In J. Cottingham, R. Stoothoff, & D. Murdoch (Trans.), *Descartes: Selected philosophical writings* (pp. 73–122). New York: Cambridge University Press. (Original work published 1641)

Dyrkton, J. (1996). Cool runnings: The coming of cyberreality in Jamaica. In R. Shields (Ed.). *Cultures of internet: Virtual spaces, real histories, living bodies* (pp. 49–57). London: Sage.

Dyson, E., Gilder, G., Keyworth, G., & Toffler, A. (1996). Cyberspace and the American dream: A magna carta for the knowledge age. *The information society, 12*(3), 295–308. (Also available at http://www.pff.org)

Gans, D., & Sirius, R. (1991, Winter). Civilizing the electronic frontier. *Mondo 2000,* pp. 48–51.

Gibson, W. (1984). *Neuromancer.* New York: Ace.

Grosz, E. (1994). *Volatile bodies: Toward a corporeal feminism.* Bloomington: Indiana University Press.

Gunkel, D., & Gunkel, A. (1997). Virtual geographies: The new worlds of cyberspace. *Critical studies in mass communications,14*(2), 123–137.

Gurak, L. (1997, May). Utopian visions of cyberspace. *Computer Mediated Communications,* pp. 1–2. Retrieved May 6, 1997 from the World Wide Web: http://www.december.com/cmc/mag/1997/may/last.html

Haraway, D. (1991). A cyborg manifesto: Science, technology, and social feminism in the late twentieth century. In D. Haraway (Ed.), *Simians, cyborgs, women: The reinvention of nature* (pp. 149–181). New York: Routledge.

Heaven's Gate. (1997). Retrieved April 9, 1997 from the World Wide Web: http://www.heavensgate.com

Hegel, G. (1987). *Encyclopedia of the philosophical sciences* (William Wallace, Trans.). New York: Oxford. (Original work published 1830)

Hillis, K. (1996). A geography of the eye: The technologies of virtual reality. In R. Shields (Ed.), *Cultures of internet: Virtual spaces, real histories, living bodies* (pp. 70–98). London: Sage.

Hoffman, D., Novak , T., & Chatterjee, P. (1996). Commercial scenarios for the web: Opportunities & challenges. Retrieved April 9, 1997 from the World Wide Web: http://www.usc.edu/dept/annenberg/vol1/issue3/hoffman.html

Interrogate the Internet. (1996). Contradictions in cyberspace: Collective response. In R. Shields (Ed.), *Cultures of internet: Virtual spaces, real histories, living bodies* (pp. 125–132). London: Sage.

Jacobson, M., & Mazur, L. (1995). *Marketing madness: A survival guide for a consumer society.* Boulder, CO: Westview.

Jordan, W. (1974). *The white man's burden.* New York: Oxford University Press.

Kroker, A., & Weinstein, M. (1994) *Data trash: The theory of the virtual class.* New York: St. Martin's.

Leder, D. (1990). *The absent body.* Chicago: University of Chicago Press.

Loraux, N. (1989). Therefore, Socrates is immortal (J. Lloyd, Trans.). In M. Feher (Ed.), *Zone 4: Fragments for a history of the human body* (pp. 12–45). New York: Zone.

MCI. (1997, January 2). [Television commercial] Channel 5 (NBC), Chicago, 7:28 p.m.

Meyers, J. (1990). *D. H. Lawrence.* New York: Knopf.

Mitchell, W. (1995). *City of bits: Space, place, and the infobahn.* Cambridge, MA: MIT Press.

Nietzsche, F. (1966). *Beyond good and evil* (W. Kaufmann, Trans.). New York: Vintage. (Original work published 1886)

Nietzsche, F. (1983). Thus spoke Zarathustra (W. Kaufmann, Trans.). In W. Kaufmann (Ed.), *The portable Nietzsche* (pp. 103–439). New York: Penguin. (Original work published 1892)

Penny, S. (1994). Virtual reality as the completion of the Enlightenment project. In G. Bender & T. Druckrey (Eds.), *Cultures on the brink: Ideologies of technology* (pp. 231–248). Seattle, WA: Bay.

Plato. (1961). *Cratylus* (B. Jowett, Trans.). In E. Hamilton & H. Cairns (Eds.), *The collected dialogues of Plato* (pp. 421–474). New York: Random House.

Plato. (1990). *Phaedo* (H. N. Fowler, Trans.). Cambridge, England: Harvard University Press.

Smith, L. (1961). *Killers of the dream.* New York: Norton.

Spelman, E. (1988). *Inessential woman: Problems of exclusion in feminist thought.* Boston: Beacon.

Spinelli, M. (1996). Radio lessons for the internet. *Postmodern culture, 6*(2) pp. 1–18. Retrieved April 21, 1997 from the World Wide Web: http://muse.jhu.edu/journals/postmodern_culture/v006/6.2spinelli.html

Stone, A. (1993). Will the real body please stand up?: Boundary stories about virtual cultures. In M. Benedikt (Ed.), *Cyberspace: First steps* (pp. 81–118). Cambridge, MA: MIT Press.

Journal of Mass Media Ethics
Volume 13, Number 2, pp. 124–136

Cases and Commentaries

The Journal of Mass Media Ethics publishes case studies in which scholars and media professionals outline how they would address a particular ethical problem. Some cases are purely hypothetical, but most are from actual experience in newsrooms, corporations, and other agencies.

We invite readers to call our attention to current cases and issues. (There is a special need for good cases in advertising and public relations.) We also invite suggestions of names of people, both professionals and academicians, who might write commentaries. Tom Cooper, professor of Visual and Media Arts at Emerson College, wrote the following case.

Lou Hodges, Editor
Knight Professor in the Ethics of Journalism
Washington and Lee University
Lexington, VA 24450
(540) 463–8786

Marketing New Software and Choreographing Intelligent Agents

Stan McGregor is confused. As senior research engineer for a major telecommunication and computer company, he is on the leading edge of developing important new technology called "choreographed intelligent agents." His synthesis of several types of software would allow his company to sell "need-fulfilling" services to clients over the Internet. Stan's invention would, for example, enable a client to tell his computer that he is lonely, and the choreographed intelligent agents would automatically produce a long list of options for the customer to relieve loneliness. Everything from a list of phone numbers of friends and relatives to a list of phone numbers of escort services, on-air psychologists, and lots more would appear on the computer screen all within 1 min.

On the one hand, Stan is happy because he may be on the verge of fame and fortune—if he and his company can only beat their competition to the market. On the other hand, Stan has struggled to identify several ethical issues, which he has listed in a memo to his supervisors. This list includes:

1. Accountability to customers and society: No one in Stan's company wants to study the possible side effects and long-term results of this invention on individual customers and the public. Stan knows that previous new technologies have been arguably linked to numerous problems such as carpel tunnel syndrome (computer keyboards), radiation poisoning (computer screens), brain tumors (possibly cellular phones), violence, and the generation gap (probably television). Stan is concerned that his company wants only to beat the competition, not to study the product's positive and negative potential.

2. Accountability to company and shareholders: The rush to success is preventing the company from seeking the level of quality control that would help the company maintain respectability. Stan is aware that America Online and other companies grew too fast to assure satisfactory customer service and quality, but he feels tremendous pressure to market mass-produced software before rival companies do. The vice presidents of sales and of research and development are talking to Stan about "heat from above."

3. Dehumanization: Stan's product will arguably change people's lives. It is just the type of technology that some people may well come to rely on rather than consulting personal advisors, clergy, partners, and family about vital decisions. Where might such pseudoadvisors lead society?

4. Privacy and protection: Aware that the Internet is easily monitored, Stan is concerned that anyone's choreographed agents could be remotely inspected. Hackers, the media, competitors, and psychopaths could find out who ordered pill, preacher, or prostitute to "relieve" loneliness. Viruses, Trojan horses, "cookies," and so forth could cause problems for Stan's clients. The company will not pay to add the right encryption and protections software as part of the package. Stan's supervisor argues that this would raise the price considerably and give an edge to the competition.

At least once per month, people like Stan and his customers contact ethicists about the ethical questions and about the "rip-off" of controversial technology they encounter. They raise such questions as the following:

(a) How much, if any, ethical responsibility do media and new technology creators and owners have to test, develop, and safeguard new technologies prior to marketing them?

(b) How much responsibility does the government have to inspect and study such new technologies, as it once did in the Office of Technology Assessment (which was dissolved by the U.S. government 3 years ago)?

(c) Should software vendors, Internet providers, and new tech developers be required to warn the public about hidden privacy encroachment and to educate users about possible viruses, Trojan horses, piracy, and online theft? Or, is this simply a case of "buyer beware?"

(d) If automation continues to "dehumanize" society, who is responsible for studying, reducing, or even preventing long-term social problems?

Commentary #1

Just a Better Mousetrap? Or Real Ethical Issues?

The hypothetical Stan McGregor may be confused, but real-life Andrew Grove is not. *Time* magazine, in its cover story marking Grove's selection as its 1997 "Man of the Year," asked the head of the world's biggest computer chip maker to discuss technology's role in society. The Intel Corporation chief's firm reply: "Technology happens. It's not good, it's not bad. Is steel good or bad?"

Hardware makers perhaps can live with the belief that technology is amoral. When powering computers that run medical devices, Intel chips help doctors save lives. When powering computers attached to the Internet, Intel chips help people peddle child pornography or pirate software. The user determines the morality.

However, it is a little harder for software makers—whether it be McGregor's company or the producer of any insipid sitcom—to escape ethical questions.

At first glance, it seems, McGregor's company has little to worry about. The company appears to be merely building a better mousetrap. The world is filled with "need-fulfillment" services—we call them the Yellow Pages, or McDonald's, or "Little Black Books," or the Yahoo! search engine on the World Wide Web. The information that McGregor's company wants to put at your fingertips is only at arm's length reach already. His company's customers are paying for convenience.

However, several concrete and abstract issues spring to mind, including the following: Who develops the list of ways to satisfy needs? If it turns commercial—if an escort service pays to have its phone number at the top of the "lonely" list—then the product is not a service at all. It is a high-tech infomercial. Separating sheep from goats is a major problem on the Internet. (Ask Pierre Salinger.) McGregor's company has an obligation—and a necessity if it wants to be successful—to tell customers how it creates its lists. Otherwise, it does not deserve to pass beyond the status of Internet snake-oil salesman.

Why is more privacy not tied into the system? Internet users are becoming sophisticated when it comes to privacy. You can buy programs to strip "cookies" from your browser. PUP lets you send encrypted e-mail that is hard to crack. You can put sensitive data on computers not physically connected to the Internet. As a practical matter, McGregor's bosses are short-sighted by ignoring security on the Web. Savvy consumers soon learn to steer clear of commercial enterprises that do not guarantee privacy. If the company will not safeguard its data on individual users, the company has an obligation to warn potential customers of privacy issues.

At what point do you give up on quality control and ship the product? Software, by its very nature, is never completed. One of the best (and worst) things about software is that you can ship it as soon as it is stable, listen to the bug reports, and fix it for the next version. By getting to market, McGregor's company will quickly learn how much more it must do to capture consumers. In addition, the "vaporware" often wins the early battle over market share. That does not make it right. Software companies walk a fine line between being first to market and selling a product that works, and their decision is quickly tested in the marketplace. (Meanwhile, a good rule of thumb for consumers: Never buy Version 1.0 of any product.)

Why should the government inspect this new technology? If it forbids the product, it seems like a case of prior restraint. Ultimately, the market-place will tell McGregor's company if it is going right or wrong. The government already has some mechanisms in place to slap down companies that go too far. Federal agencies have chased down medical quacks who have set up shop online. In addition, if McGregor's company turns into a escort referral service, expect prosecutors to step in.

Who decides where the line crosses from convenience into "dehumanization?" The government? Software reviewers? The Unabomber? The answer, of course, is the humans who use the product. It is important to remember that, for every person who has embraced computers and the Internet, at least one other person either does not care or gave it up as boring, slow, or silly. In fact, you can argue that McGregor's software ultimately is humanizing. If you are lonely, then it gives you a list of people to talk to. Worries about "dehumanization" began long before personal computers and the Internet. Henry Ford made cheap cars that let people quickly leave their neighborhood. Filo Farnsworth chipped in with a television set. Milton Berle gave people a reason to stay inside on Sunday nights instead of sitting outside on the front porch. The ultimate choice remains up to consumers. Nobody forces you to watch television or fire up the Internet. You decide how human or "dehuman" you want to be. Maybe Andrew Grove is more right than we know.

By Chris Roberts
Editor and Reporter
The Birmingham News

Commentary #2

Stan has Three Categories of Concerns

Good for Stan! He is to be heartily commended for his concerns about the potential effects of his product on a variety of constituencies. It would be pleasant to imagine him in the company of a large number of ethically sensitive, or even cognizant, software developers—but it seems doubtful.

However, Stan would be less likely to be ignored (at best) by his evil, money-grubbing bosses if he calms down and makes himself a little list dividing his concerns into three categories: those that he or his company can effectively address, those that would be better tackled at the industry level, and those that either are aspects of computer use in general or are so tenuously linked to any negative effects that they should be set aside until more evidence is in.

The biggest issue he can actually do something about—and can pitch convincingly to his bosses—is privacy. Good ethics and good business coincide on this one. Privacy repeatedly shows up at the top of the list when Web users cite their concerns about the medium. Failure to declare very publicly that this new software, designed to collect sensitive personal information about individuals, will seek to safeguard that information from unwelcome use would be a poor, even potentially fatal, business decision. Privacy protection is not just a strong selling point; its absence could doom the product. Besides, by pledging to honor users' privacy, Stan's firm has an opportunity to be welcomed into the company of prestigious technology manufacturers, who in December 1997 unveiled a voluntary code of conduct in this area. The Information Technology Industry Council, which includes PC makers such as Dell and chip makers such as Intel, came up with eight principles in response to President Clinton's call for the industry to protect privacy through self-regulation. Among other things, the guidelines recommend that a company tell users what personal data are being collected and allow them to specify how data are used. For instance, no cookies unless we know they are there.

One simple, quick, and cheap option for Stan's company would be to take advantage of the labeling system implemented last summer by eTRUST, a global consumer privacy initiative backed by such industry giants as AT&T, Excite, IBM, and Netscape. Under that system, Web sites display "trustmarks" notifying users of their privacy policies. In other words, full public disclosure about how information will be used is made up front. Stan's software presumably works by matching individual needs, so it may not be eligible for the top "No Exchange" label, which means that a site uses no personally identifiable information. However, it might qualify for a "One-to-One Exchange" trust mark, indicating that a site does collect data but only for the site owner's use. The company vows that information will not be shared with or sold to anyone else. A better, though more expensive, approach would be to incorporate encryption software within the program itself. Stan apparently has not gotten very far in his push for encryption, but again, he may have more success appealing to his bosses' business sense. Computer users tend to be more concerned about privacy than about incremental software costs. They are sure to have misgivings about the security of what they tell these agents—potentially so many misgivings that they will refuse to buy the software at all without protection.

Moving beyond privacy, Stan's realm of influence allows him to push for packaging and promotion that includes a prominent explanation of exactly what this software can and cannot do for people. It won't make users popular, sexy, or acne-free. It won't even make them less lonely. What it will do is offer them options for making human contact; the choice of whether and how to use it will be theirs. Stan falls under the category of sound business ethics: being honest in marketing a product and in communicating with customers, especially vulnerable ones.

Granted, these may not be easy sells, especially if they delay the product launch. However, from an ethical standpoint, the choice between accountability to customers and accountability to shareholders is something of a no-brainer. Do you take action to avoid doing harm (to a potentially large number of people, if Stan wants to make a utilitarian argument)? Or, do you take action to boost financial profit (to a relatively small group)? Like most choices in which greed (for which loyalty to shareholders is a not infrequent stand-in in the corporate world) drives one side of the argument, it is an easy ethical decision. The rush to market raises ethical concerns—in the news business no less than in any other business. Stan's best strategy would be to present the sound ethical decision as the sound business decision. In this case, it is. Testing, developing, and safeguarding new technologies are all things he can lobby for within his company. He may not win unless the standard procedure of the industry as a whole changes. This can happen if issues best addressed by an industry group which give them a wider voice are brought to public consciousness. These are social issues stemming from computer use and potential abuse or misuse. Computer Professionals for Social Responsibility is another group Stan could contact or join. Or, he could work to form new coalitions among software developers who share his concerns.

As a single employee in a single company, he is likely to get thrown to the sharks. As an interest group backed by the strength of numbers of similarly concerned and knowledgeable insiders, his concerns are more likely to gain the hearing necessary for them to become topics of public debate, or at least awareness. He can then work for real change instead of merely playing Don Quixote to the corporate treadmill. Solo action may be existentially noble, and Stan is free to put his job on the line over his concerns. However, such an approach is almost surely going to fail to get the issues addressed or even publicly talked about. In addition, Stan is going to be unemployed, losing not just his job but his computer-industry insider's leverage. At the top of this list should be Stan's concerns about potentially dehumanizing and isolating effects of his product. The problem of social disconnection is not new; no single technology is to blame for it, and no single technology can solve it. Does software such as Stan's isolate individuals or connect them? Does the Web fragment society or unite it? The answers seem to be "yes." However, despite the ambiguities, this is a very real issue, one much bigger than Stan's intelligent agent software and one that begs for serious consideration by techno-savvy ethicists as well as by users of these interactive technologies. To apply Sissela Bok's simple model, these are not issues Stan can resolve by consulting his own conscience or appealing to the moral sense of his bosses. In addition, consultation among his peers in the software industry is not enough by itself. However, he and his peers can be agents for submitting the issue to the ethical scrutiny that will come through public awareness, public discussion, and public input.

It also is at this level that Stan can effectively raise his concerns about privacy issues in general: viruses, Trojan horses, piracy, and the rest. These go beyond individual-level concerns about his software in particular. They are issues that a large number of people are thinking and talking about. Stan is obviously a connected kind of guy; he should tap into and contribute to that lively, ongoing discourse. Stan also wonders if the government, presumably the U.S. government, has a responsibility in this area. If so, Washington is woefully ill-equipped to meet it. Effective action relating to this global medium requires international cooperation. Getting all the governments of the world to agree on anything is problematic; getting them to do it in a timely fashion is laughable. By the time even one government gets around to studying a new technology, it is already six generations behind. Governments are prone to want to move on to the next step: regulation. In the current political environment, even Washington is pushing the computer industry toward self-regulation rather than government regulation—toward ethics, that is, rather than law.

Finally, some of Stan's concerns have to be set aside lest he start to sound like a boy crying wolf. Ethics is about making choices, and one choice involves picking fights wisely; he risks undermining concerns about software, an area that needs his expertise and ethical sensitivity, by harping on every possible risk. Carpal tunnel syndrome may or may not be a side effect of improper computer use. (The problems seem to result from prolonged typing with insufficient ergonomic support and inadequate breaks. The purpose of his intelligent agent software is to get people away from the computer.) Serious as these illnesses are, a cause-and-effect relation between them and computer use may never be proven. Hardware manufacturers will be better equipped to deal with it than will Stan or other developers of individual pieces of software, no matter how compelling. He also may want to set aside the relation between violence and computer use as an issue to which his expertise simply does not apply. Besides, it is a can of worms, as TV executives know all too well. First, there are the free speech issues; the ratings system is too new for us to know if it will have a chilling effect on TV programming, but the possibility certainly exists. Then, there are the difficulties of proving any sort of direct causal relation between violence and media use. Researchers have been trying for years, with debatable success. If I were Stan, I would stay well away.

As a quick footnote, in addition to ethical concerns, there are some possible legal niceties that Stan may want to lie awake nights worrying about. There is, for instance, a difference between ordering up a preacher and ordering up a prostitute—or, depending on the kind of pill it is, a pill. As the poor slobs who have been hauled off to jail for downloading child pornography from the Web have discovered, possession of illegal materials is more than nine tenths of the law. Even if the software does not include, say, hookers on its lists (and so-called escort services are iffy) when they leave the shelves, it will not take folks long to figure out how to add them, using the same personalization features that let them bring up phone numbers of friends and relatives. Legal limits are difficult to identify online, and net law is in state of flux. However, Stan should again think seriously about pushing for a high-visibility disclaimer. There's nothing like a well-publicized court case to dampen profits.

By Jane B. Singer
Assistant Professor of Journalism
Colorado State University

Commentary #3

The Big Issues: Liability, Quality Control, and Security

Sounds like Stan and his company have problems, big problems. If they are not having conversations about the ethical issues Stan is nervous about and if the focus in all their development and marketing is on the technology, then they probably are not having conversations on the even greater concerns of liability, quality control, and security. In a marketplace in which customer loyalty changes weekly with the latest "hot site" designation, a service such as Stan's company is proposing raises a lot of issues about ensuring a site that an increasingly savvy consumer marketplace will buy.

The product, this "choreographed intelligent agent," sounds like the ultimate in one-to-one marketing, and it has the potential of being a great service—a combination of personal yellow pages, self-help book, and friend with the right connections. Technology, which can reveal more about you with each transaction and can be customized to fit your needs, just might be the consumer service of the future: Type in "hungry" and get the menus of nearby restaurants, dial in grocery shopping and delivery services, a recipe database. The possibilities seem endless, and useful, but Stan and his partners must consider the following before they market the service.

> ## The engine is the smallest part of the concern.

Stan's concern about accountability to the customers and society is warranted but less on ethical or moral grounds and more on the legal ones. What liability will the company have if the dating service a lonely customer is pointed to turns out to be a scam and cheats him out of thousands of dollars? What if the take-out food he gets on the service's advice gives him food poisoning? Stan must be sure he looks into issues about how the company is marketing the service. The positive factor of this aspect of Stan's concern—the potential to help people live broader, more informed lives—is great. Needing to protect the company from legal implications, however, is great too.

The concern Stan has about the company's haste to market the new service is highly warranted. The engine that runs a service such as this is the smallest part of the concern; it is the content the engine drives that is of utmost importance. Issues about quality control—such as data refreshing (is the latest information there? what is the soup of the day at that restaurant?), spot checks of the validity and viability of services being linked to, and the ability to update the personal profile of customers—better be in place before the service is introduced. The first time a customer is sent to a dead link, or gets information not suited to his or her personal needs, will be the last time he or she uses the service (there will be seven more services just announced to which she can go!).

The dehumanization factor Stan worries about is of the least concern. This service is a tool of facilitation, and it will possibly lead to higher interaction with qualified advisors. There are people behind the finder service. If this service has excellent selection and quality control, leading customers to the most highly qualified, reliable, and credible sources, then people will be greatly benefitted in their search for advisors and support. The links people can make to people through the network can be an electronic hand reaching out. This is not a case of either–or. The service, presumably, would lead the client to local sources of aid and advice, such as clergy. The lonely customer could get a gentle reminder to think about giving his sister a call and pull her number out of his personal Rolodex. The concern here is whether the listings in the service lead only to those services or "advisors" who pay a fee to be part of the listing and for whom there is no credibility check. If the service is like those vanity "expert" directors, essentially paid ads for fringe "experts," then savvy customers will quickly see through it. Stan needs to worry about such content issues of the service.

Privacy concerns are the battle front on which Stan should muster his troops. If the company does not provide adequate encryption and protection software, it is doomed to a grand opening with no customers. People are getting smarter about security, and the reviewers of new sites will report on the relative security of the service as part of their evaluations. Word of mouth, quickly passed in the newsgroups and listservs, will doom the service if those concerns are not addressed.

The bottom line is that the best offense is a good defense, and citizens in this burgeoning information age are learning some truly important defensive skills: How to protect themselves, how to make value judgments about information and services, and how to identify and choose among the best available services. I think it is part of journalists' ethical responsibility not only to understand these issues themselves but also to inform their readers, viewers, listeners, and "clickers."

By Nora Paul
Poynter Institute for Media Studies

Commentary #4

Ethical Action and Emerging Technologies:
Between a Rock and a Hard Place?

If asked to identify core ethical issues, many individuals would no doubt mention fostering a good society and doing what is right. It would also be recognized that everyone periodically faces ethical choices in which values conflict and in which what the right thing to do is not always immediately obvious. The work of information and computer professionals abounds with opportunities to do the right thing when designing, developing, or implementing software and facilitating its effective use. Stan's quandary, therefore, is an unenviable but all too common one for a software designer.

Here are his options: to release what may potentially be the next "killer app" ahead of the curve and hope to beat the competition (trusting that the product will be used in socially responsible ways) or to invest time and money in testing—tracking and checking bugs, plugging security holes— and attempt to help the nontechnical laity comprehend the implications of the product's use (and run the risk of diminished profitability due to higher unit cost or late market entry).

Stan's apprehension over employer pressure to release his choreographed intelligent agent software too early and untested illustrates not only the more self-evident ethical issues of his dilemma but also hints at a deeper level of concern he otherwise ignores.

First of all, Stan is reported to have synthesized several types of existing software in order to develop the new product. Certainly, producing new software by building on existing programs is nothing new. However, if Stan anticipates that users of the new software will be the existing client base, if the new product incorporates a look and feel similar to that of existing products, and if the new product advertisements stressed its compatibility with existing products, then we might question Stan's ethics. Were his actions ethical or ethically compromised? If Stan is trustworthy and acted honestly, honoring property rights (including copyrights and patents) and giving proper credit (including meeting fiduciary obligations) for intellectual property used to create the new software, then we can say that this aspect of the case meets ethical standards. Unfortunately, we are not given enough information to make this judgment with confidence.

Second, the inherent complexity of most computer software makes it easy to illustrate the importance of ethical choices when presented with dramatic cases of people who can be hurt by poor choices (especially in safety-critical systems). Computer software affects an increasingly large number of people and presents a potential threat that is difficult to control because it is dispersed and noncentralized. Perhaps because of this the media have found it easy to energize moral dramas against small groups of hacker bad guys who try to tap into computer systems in order to access sensitive data. They make it easy to vilify reclusive teenage computer geniuses who develop novel viruses and Trojan horses that trash data and bring entire computer systems crashing down. Less often reported, although no less insidious, are the corporate encroachments on personal freedom and privacy afforded by new developments in computing software (e.g., undocumented but built-in requirements to use certain network access software while deleting a rival's unsolicited spamming of e-mail lists, or using "magic cookies" to track web browser access and view client preferences). Enveloped within such a social milieu, Stan must face the ethical uncertainty that results from wondering whose points of view to consider in the design and release of a new computer application: the views of the potential users of the software (the customers) or those of his employer (the company and its shareholders). What does "do the right thing" mean in this case?

If one were to employ the perspectives of philosopher John Rawls (1971), one might ask Stan to identify all the key participants, including technical staff, computer users, and so on and determine whether his software could pass the following two tests (adapted from Collins, Miller, Spielman, & Wherry, 1994):

1. Will the software increase harm to the least advantaged? It would be ill-advised to release a software product if it increased the potential of harming ill-informed users who might already be vulnerable to that kind of (financial or personal) harm.

2. Will tradeoffs between financial benefit to one party (the company) and personal harm to another party (the customer), if made public, cause outrage to most members of society? In other words, do not make decisions you could not defend with honor before an informed public.

Of course, many professional organizations—for instance, the Association for Computing Machinery (ACM)—have adopted codes of ethics and codes of conduct that derive from universal ethical injunctions (e.g., avoid harm to others) and tend to carry the weight of quasilegal force. Of particular relevance to the present case would be the following items of the ACM (1993) code:

- Contribute to society and human well-being;
- Avoid harm to others;
- Respect the privacy of others;
- Give comprehensive and thorough evaluations of computer systems and their impacts, including analysis of possible risks; and
- Improve public understanding of computing and its consequences.

Corporations with quick-acting, aggressive, macho management styles—like those Stan seems to be under—tend to encourage the taking of ethical risks. If they engage in ethical misconduct, it would appear unlikely that a professional association like the ACM would be able to discipline them effectively.

Finally, Stan and his supervisors appear to be blind to the fact that they are developing not merely a software product for mass consumption but a medium. Computer-based communications can be a catalyst for widespread social change. The medium depends as strongly on social attitudes and ethical conduct as it does on technology (hardware, software, netware). It is ultimately driven by the dynamic between these forces. Computer Professionals for Social Responsibility (CPSR) has developed principles that stress the need for a consensus that will govern how society will come to terms with this new medium. The principles also place people firmly in the role of stewards—not owners—of the Net (Borenstein, 1998). What Stan seems to understand, but his superiors need to learn, is that society has an interest in the Internet that supersedes the economic interest of those who build, maintain, and provide the means of access to it. Although their need to earn a profit must be respected, they, in return, must respect the fact that the larger needs of society may place limits on their own economic interests.

By Michael R. Ogden
Assistant Professor of Communications
University of Hawaii at Manoa

References

Association for Computing Machinery. (1993, February). Code of ethics and professional conduct (1992). *Communications of the ACM*, pp. 99–103.

Borenstein, N. (1998, Winter). One planet, one net, many voices: The development of SPCR's Principles for the Internet Era. *CPSR Newsletter*, pp. 1, 5–8.

Collins, W., Miller, K., Spielman, B., & Wherry, P. (1994, January). How good is good enough? An ethical analysis of software construction and its use. *Communications of the ACM*, pp. 39–48.

Rawls, J. (1971). *A theory of justice*. Cambridge, MA: Harvard University Press.